Drawings in Greek and Roman Architecture

Antonio Corso

Archaeopress Archaeology

ARCHAEOPRESS PUBLISHING LTD
GORDON HOUSE
276 BANBURY ROAD
OXFORD OX2 7ED

www.archaeopress.com

ISBN 978 1 78491 371 7
ISBN 978 1 78491 372 4 (e-Pdf)

© Archaeopress and A Corso 2016

Cover: P. Oxy. LXXI 4842 The upper sections of two Corinthian unfluted columns with their capitals are represented, as well as an architrave with upper taenia and a frieze with a decoration of shoots of acanthus: from an Oxyrhynchus Papyrus of around AD 140.

All rights reserved. No part of this book may be reproduced, stored in retrieval system, or transmitted, in any form or by any means, electronic, mechanical, photocopying or otherwise, without the prior written permission of the copyright owners.

This book is available direct from Archaeopress or from our website www.archaeopress.com

Contents

Abstract v

Introduction 1

1. The treatises written by architects about specific architectural works made by them 4

2. The illustrations which accompanied the text of the *de architectura* by Vitruvius 15

3. Drawings included in handbooks after Vitruvius. 26

4. Images attached to ancient descriptions of architecture 28

5. Miniature illustrations in Gromatic treatises. 34

6. References to architectural drawings in ancient literatures and inscriptions ... 36

7. Archaeological evidence of drawings of architecture 40

8. Conclusions. 48
    I. Chronology of the evidence. 48
    II. What drawings of architecture looked like. 50
    III. Functions of architectural drawings 51
    IV. Critical deductions. 52

9. Catalogue of drawings of architecture in the Greek and Roman world. ... 53

List of Figures

1. Drawing from the temple of Athena at Priene from Koenigs (note 109). 54
2. Drawings from the Didymaion from Haselberger (note 110) 55
3. Drawings from the Didymaion from Haselberger (note 110) 56
4. Drawings from the Didymaion from Haselberger (note 110) 57
5. Drawings from the Didymaion from Haselberger (note 110) 58
6. Drawings from the Didymaion from Haselberger (note 110) 59
7. Drawings from the Didymaion from Haselberger (note 110) 60
8. Drawings from the Didymaion from Haselberger (note 110) 61
9. Drawings from the Didymaion from Haselberger (note 110) 62
10. Drawings from the Iseum of Philae from Heisel (note 109) 63
11. Drawings from the Iseum of Philae from Heisel (note 109) 64
12. Drawing from the temple of Horus at Edfu from Heisel (note 109). 65
13. Drawings from Susa from Heisel (note 109). 66
14. Drawings from Susa from Heisel (note 109). 67
15. Drawings from the temple of Mandulis at Bab–al–Kalabsha from Heisel (note 109). 68
16. Drawings from the temple of Mandulis at Bab–al–Kalabsha from Heisel (note 109). 69
17. Drawings from Gebel Abu Foda from Heisel (note 109)... 70
18. Drawings from Gebel Abu Foda from Heisel (note 109)... 71
19. Drawing from Meroe from Heisel (note 109). 72
20. Drawing from the papyrus of Oxyrhynchus 2406 from Haselberger (note 110). 73
21. Drawing from the papyrus of Oxyrhynchus 4842 from Coulton (note 133) 74
22. Drawings from Bziza from Heisel (note 109). 75
23. Drawings from Bziza from Heisel (note 109). 76
24. Drawings from Baalbek from Lohmann (note 138) 77
25. Drawings from Baalbek from Lohmann (note 138) 78
26a. Drawings from Baalbek from Lohmann (note 138) 79
26b. Drawings from Baalbek from Lohmann (note 138) 80
27. Drawings from Baalbek from Lohmann (note 138) 81
28. Drawings from Baalbek from Lohmann (note 138) 82
29. Drawings from the terrace of the theatre of Pergamum from Heisel (note 109) and Haselberger (note 110). 83
30. Drawings from the terrace of the theatre of Pergamum from Heisel (note 109) and Haselberger (note 110). 84

31. Drawings from the court in front of the Mausoleum of Augustus at Rome from Haselberger (note 141) 85

32. Drawings from the court in front of the Mausoleum of Augustus at Rome from Haselberger (note 141) 86

33. Drawings from the large Amphitheater of Capua from Heisel (note 109) 87

34. Drawings from the large Amphitheater of Capua from Heisel (note 109) 88

35. Drawings from the large Amphitheater of Capua from Heisel (note 109) 89

36. Drawing from the Amphitheater of Pola from Haselberger (note 110) 90

37. Drawing from Thysdrus at Bern from Loertscher (note 145) 91

38. Fragment of marble panel from Via Anicia at Rome from Tucci (note 148). 92

39. Fragment of marble panel from the Oppius hill at Rome from Meneghini and Santangeli Valenzani (note 148). 93

40. Marble panel from the Forum of Nerva at Rome, *ibidem*. 94

41. Marble panel at Urbino, Lapidario del Palazzo Ducale, and restitution drawing of the represented Mausoleum by Huelsen, *ibidem*. 95

42. Marble panel at Urbino, Lapidario del Palazzo Ducale, and restitution drawing of the represented Mausoleum by Huelsen, *ibidem*. 96

43. Marble panel of Perugia, Museo Archeologico, and restitution drawing of the represented Mausoleum by Huelsen, *ibidem*. 97

44. Marble panel of Perugia, Museo Archeologico, and restitution drawing of the represented Mausoleum by Huelsen, *ibidem*. 98

45. Marble panel from Portus, *ibidem*. 99

46. Marble panel *quondam* at Amelia, *ibidem*. 100

47. Drawing restitution of the Severan *forma Urbis* with the surviving fragments in their original places, *ibidem*. 101

48. Marble panel of the Forum of Augustus, *ibidem*. 103

49. Plan of *Aguntum,* from Heisel (note 109). 104

50. Plan of aqueduct from the Aventinus hill, from Heisel (note 109). 105

51. Mosaic with drawing of baths from Via Marsala at Roma, from Heisel (note 109). 106

52. Mosaic with drawing of funerary enclosure from Ostia, from Heisel (note 109). 107

53. Mosaic with drawing of circus from Luni, House of Mosaics, from Meneghini and Santangeli Valenzani (note 148). 108

54. Drawing of rotunda from Pompeii, Casa del Citarista, from De Vos (note 155). 110

55. Drawing of capital from Pompeii, Casa di Cerere, from De Vos (note 156). 111

Abstract

The aim of this study is the survey of all the evidence, both visual and written, related to ancient drawings with architectural contents in the ancient Greek and Roman world.

An introductory chapter provides preliminary information about ancient architectural drawings and gives a short history of the consideration of this issue in the scholarly world.

A first chapter concerns the treatises written by ancient Greek architects about monuments they built. The ancient evidence concerning these books is analytically considered and the question as to whether these books included drawings of the described projects is discussed.

A second chapter concerns the illustrations which were included in the *de architectura* by Vitruvius but did not survive in the manuscript tradition. The problem of understanding what these drawings looked like is considered.

Then a third chapter concerns the possibility that other treatises about architectural matters after Vitruvius were provided with illustrating drawings.

A fourth chapter focuses the literary genre of the descriptions of architecture in the Greek and Roman world: the issue as to whether these evocations of monuments were accompanied by drawings is thoroughly discussed.

The fifth chapter concerns another literary genre: that of the so-called 'gromatic' writings, *i.e.* of treatises concerning agricultural colonies of the Roman world. In the manuscript tradition, these treatises are accompanied by miniature representations of a few colonies.

The possible relationship of these illustrations with drawings of buildings in books on architectural matters is discussed.

The sixth chapter is a collection of the literary and epigraphical references to drawings of architecture: in most cases, these drawings were projects submitted by architects to landowners or patrons of monuments to be built.

The seventh chapter is a survey of the archaeological evidence of this genre of drawing.

The above outlined systematic presentation of the evidence concerning architectural drawings leads to the establishment of a chronological sequence of the collected material. Moreover the issue about how projects' drawings looked like is investigated. A list of functions justifying the surviving architectural drawings is attempted.

Critical conclusions about how these drawings shed light on the status of architects and craftsmen in antiquity as well as concerning the existence of drawings with artistic purposes in antiquity are suggested.

Finally a catalogue of a *corpus* of 55 ancient drawings of architectural patterns is provided: all the items of the catalogue are illustrated.

The visual evidence included in this catalogue ranges from the 4th c. BC to AD 5th c. and has been found in monuments from Asia Minor, Mesopotamia, the Syrian region, Egypt, Rome and central Italy, northern Africa, Hystria and *Noricum*.

The architecture on which these figures are incised include temples, amphitheaters, burial monuments and quarries, while some examples are found on marble and clay mobile supports as well as on papyri.

It is hoped that this book will make use of the above considered evidence easier for scholars to access, thus promoting scholarly discussion about architectural drawings in antiquity.

Introduction

The aim of this essay is to study the drawings of architecture in the Greek and Roman World.

While there is a huge bibliography about built architecture and at least partially preserved buildings of the classical past, the interest of scholars for drawings of architecture has been much smaller.

This fact is due to the circumstance that until a few decades ago very few drawings of buildings had been noticed. Moreover these representations were not very impressive and could easily be thought to constitute a 'minor' genre of visual evidence of the ancient world.

This prejudice has no reason to exist because, as will be shown below, the drawings were salient and meaningful moments of the architectural activity in ancient times from several view points: projects of buildings usually were shown and visualized through drawings, moreover craftsmen often employed in building activities incised on walls drawings of the architectural elements to be done. It is necessary to specify that not always are these sketches of high quality: however they are crucial documents in order to understand how building enterprises worked at the times and in given regions.

Moreover the use of drawings was adopted systematically by state administrations, especially at Rome, in order to represent buildings subjected to taxation as well as to make land registers.

Sometimes, legal acts concerning property of real estate also contained drawings of these buildings.

The 'free' drawing of architecture for artistic reasons is rarely evidenced, as will be shown below, but a couple of documents suggest that even this genre of drawings existed.

Finally with the decline of the ancient world, the nostalgia for monuments of the past probably leads to the creation of drawings of renowned architecture, which are targeted by art tourism. In these cases drawings had the function of modern souvenirs.

These few anticipations are meant to suggest the importance of this visual genre in the ancient culture and thus to justify the followings pages.

The importance of drawings in the architectural activity of the Hellenistic world had been brought to the attention of the scholarly community especially by Lothar Haselberger, who throughout the 1980s and 1990s of last century published the most important construction drawings of the Didymaion (for a list of his relevant publications, see note 110). The notion that drawings were a necessary step toward the making of a building led to the publication of a *corpus* of architectural drawings in the ancient world: this catalog was made by Joachim P. Heisel, *Antike Bauzeichnungen*, Darmstadt (1993). Heisel's catalog was very important, moreover it has not been substituted by a more recent one and thus even now is a useful research tool: in this essay it is cited often.

However during the last decades the archaeological evidence of architectural drawings became richer thanks to new discoveries. Moreover, in Heisel's book the references to architectural drawings in epigraphic and literary *testimonia* did not receive enough consideration.

Finally, there are literary genres which have to do with architectural drawings and had not been treated in that worthy book: these literary branches are the treatises of architects about their own creations, Vitruvius' handbook about architecture, the descriptive or ekphrastic literature and finally the gromatic treatises. On the contrary the scientific need to consider these themes for a better understanding of the origins and of the fortune of architectural drawings in the Greek and Roman world is one of the reasons which justify this new book.

Finally the publication of the papyrus of Artemidorus led the renowned scholar Salvatore Settis (see note 1) to a revaluation of the art of drawing as an important branch of the visual arts of the ancient world. Although Settis focused especially on drawing as a preliminary moment in the making of painting and sculpture, the understanding of the phenomenon of drawing architecture is crucial also in order to appreciate the various functions of drawings in the ancient visual culture.

This essay has been written in the years 2014 and 2015 thanks to a contract from the Center of Vitruvian Studies based in Fano (Italy). I wish to thank Prof. Salvatore Settis, Prof. Pierre Gros, Prof. Paolo Clini, the Count Luciano Filippo Bracci, Dr. Dino Zacchilli and many other scholars who made this institution a very 'nutritious' centre of learning.

Thanks are due also to Mark Wilson Jones and Nigel Spivey because they agreed to read a preliminary version of this book and to provide comments.

Athens, 9 October, 2015

Antonio Corso

Introduction

Drawing images was a widespread practice in the ancient world.[1]

However the evidence concerning drawings of architecture has never been the object of a comprehensive and organic research.

Filling this gap in the studies of the visual culture of the ancient world is exactly the purpose of this essay.

---

[1] See S. Settis, 'Il contributo del papiro alla storia dell'arte antica', C. Gallazzi *et alii* (a c. di), *Il Papiro di Artemidoro*, Milano (2008) 579-610.

1. The treatises written by architects about specific architectural works made by them

First of all, it is necessary to study the treatises written by architects about their important architectural enterprises (usually temples). The most detailed information about these books is given by Vitruvius, *De architectura* 7. *Praefatio* 10-18:

(10) (…) omnibus scriptoribus infinitas ago gratias quod egregiis ingeniorum sollertiis ex aevo conlatis abundantes alius alio genere copias praeparaverunt, unde nos uti fontibus haurientes aquam et ad propria proposita traducentes facundiores et expeditiores habemus ad scribendum facultates talibusque confidentes auctoribus audemus institutiones novas comparare.

(11) Igitur tales ingressus eorum quia ad propositi mei rationes animadverti praeparatos, inde sumendo progredi coepi. namque primum Agatharchus Athenis Aeschylo docente tragoediam scaenam fecit et de ea commentarium reliquit. ex eo moniti Democritus et Anaxagoras de eadem re scripserunt, quemadmodum oporteat ad aciem oculorum radiorumque extentionem certo loco centro constituto lineas ratione naturali respondere, uti de incerta re certae imagines aedificiorum in scaenarum picturis redderent speciem et quae in directis planisque frontibus sint figurata, alia abscedentia alia prominentia esse videantur.

(12) Postea Silenus de symmetriis doricorum edidit volumen, de aede Iunonis quae est Sami dorica Theodorus, de ionica Ephesi quae est Dianae Chersiphron et Metagenes, de fano Minervae quod est Prienae ionicum Pytheos, item de aede Minervae dorica quae est Athenis in arce Ictinos et Carpion, Theodorus Phocaeus de tholo qui est Delphis, Philo de aedium sacrarum symmetriis et de armamentario quod fecerat Piraeei portu, Hermogenes de aede Dianae ionica quae est Magnesiae pseudodipteros et Liberi Patris Teo monopteros, item Arcesius de symmetriis corinthiis et ionico Trallibus Aesculapio quod etiam ipse sua manu dicitur fecisse, de Mausoleo Satyrus et Pytheos, quibus vero felicitas maximum summumque contulit munus.

(13) (…)

(14) Praeterea minus nobiles multi praecepta symmetriarum conscripserunt, uti Nexaris Theocydes Demophilos Pollis Leonidas Silanion Melampus Sarnacus Euphranor. non minus de machinationibus, uti Diades Archytas Archimedes Ctesibios Nymphodorus Philo Byzantius Diphilos Democles Charias Polyidos Pyrros Agesistratos. quorum ex commentariis quae utilia esse his rebus

animadverti, collecta in ea re ab Graecis volumina plura edita, ab nostris oppido quam pauca. Fuficius enim mirum de his rebus primus instituit edere volumen, item Terentius Varro de novem disciplinis unum de architectura, P. Septimius duo.

(15) Amplius vero in id genus scripturae adhuc nemo incubuisse videtur, cum fuissent et antiqui cives magni architecti, qui potuissent non minus eleganter scripta comparare. (…)

(18) Cum ergo et antiqui nostri inveniantur non minus quam Graeci fuisse magni architecti et nostra memoria satis multi, et ex his pauci praecepta edidissent, non putavi silendum sed disposite singulis voluminibus de singulis exponendum[2]

(10) I owe great gratitude to all those who with an ocean of intellectual services which they gathered from all time, each in his department provided stores from which we, like those who draw water from a spring and use it for their own purposes, have gained the means of writing with more eloquence and readiness; and trusting in such authorities we venture to put together a new manual of architecture.

(11) Because, then, I observed that such beginnings had been made towards the method of my undertaking, I drew upon these sources and began to go forward. For to begin with: Agatharchus at Athens, when Aeschylus was presenting a tragedy, was in control of the stage, and wrote a commentary about it. Following his suggestions, Democritus and Anaxagoras wrote upon the same topic, in order to show how, if a fixed centre is taken for the outward glance of the eyes and the projection of the radii, we must follow these lines in accordance with a natural law, such that from an uncertain object, uncertain images may give the appearance of buildings in the scenery of the stage, and how what is figured upon vertical and plane surfaces can seem to recede in one part and project in another.

(12) Subsequently Silenus published a work upon Doric proportions; Theodorus on the Doric temple of Juno which is at Samos; Chersiphron and Metagenes on the Ionic temple of Diana which is at Ephesus; Pythius on the temple of Minerva in the Ionic style which is at Priene; Ictinus and Carpion on the Doric temple of Minerva which is on the Acropolis at Athens; Theodorus of Phocaea on the tholos at Delphi; Philo on the proportions of temples and the arsenal which was in the harbor of the Piraeus; Hermogenes on the pseudodipteral Ionic temple of Diana at Magnesia and the monopteral temple of Father Bacchus at Teos; Arcesius on Corinthian proportions, and the Ionic temple at Tralles to Aesculapius, whose image is said to have been carved by him; Satyrus and Pythius on the Mausoleum. And on these last, good fortune conferred the greatest and highest boon.

---

[2] About this passage, see P. Gros (a c. di), *Vitruvio de architectura*, Torino (1997) 1021-1027.

(13) (…)

(14) In addition to these, many men of less fame have compiled the rule of symmetry, such as Nexaris, Theocydes, Demophilus, Pollis, Leonidas, Silanion, Melampus of Sarnaca, Euphranor. Others have written on machinery: Diades, Archytas, Archimedes, Ctesibius, Nymphodorus, Philo of Byzantium, Diphilus, Democles, Chaerias, Polyidus, Pyrrhus, Agesistratus. As to the useful contributions to our subject which I found in their commentaries, many volumes have been published by the Greeks, exceedingly few by our own writers. For Fufidius curiously enough was the first to publish a volume on these topics. Further, Varro included one volume in his work On the Nine Disciplines; Publius Septimius wrote two volumes.

(15) Up to now no one seems to have gone further in this kind of writing, although our citizens of old have been great architects who might have compiled works of equal precision.

(…)

(18) While, therefore, our predecessors are found, no less than the Greeks, to have been great architects, and sufficiently many in our own time, few of them have published their methods. Hence I thought we ought not to remain silent, but we should set forth methodically the various branches of the subject in separate volumes.' (transl. Loeb with amendments)

Vitruvius divides the 'technical' literature of the architectural field into 5 branches:

    a. treatises of scenography and perspective (sect. 11).
    b. treatises about specific architectural creations, usually temples (sect. 12).
    c. treatises about symmetry (sect. 14).
    d. treatises about machines (sect. 14).
    e. treatises on architectural subjects written by Romans in Latin (sect. 14).

The older of these specializations is that of architects who wrote treatises on architectural works made by them (branch b).

In fact this tradition harked back to the high archaic period and in particular to the greatest Ionic artist of that age: Theodorus of Samus.[3]

Vitruvius specifies that he wrote a volume about the temple of Hera on Samus and that this building was Doric. Of course he referred to the large dipterus Heraion

---

[3]See S. Ebbinghaus, 'Theodoros (I)', R. Vollkommer (ed.), *Kuenstlerlexikon der Antike*, Munich 2 (2004) 445-447.

of Samus:[4] there are two phases of this dipterus temple. Usually Theodorus and Rhoecus are thought to have made a project of the first of these two dipteri, which is called Heraion iii and is dated around 560 BC.[5] Around 530 BC the tyrant of Samus, Polycrates, promoted the definitive phase of the Heraion, which is called Heraion iv, and was never finished.[6] Since the treatise of Theodorus is supposed to have been published after the completion of the building which is the concern of this book, this treatise must have described, explained and commented on the Heraion iii and not the unfinished Heraion iv.

The specification that the temple was Doric was wrong, because these dipteri were Ionic.

However, two previous phases of that temple also existed (Heraion i and ii)[7] and it is likely that a specific architectural order was not yet adopted for them. Thus in a later period they may have been regarded 'Doric' because this was the most simple order of columns as well as the oldest.

Of course Theodorus must have written as well about the Heraion which preceded the first dipterus temple.

The invention of the dipterus temple must have been a very important innovation to justify the publication of a pamphlet in order to explain that marvel.

One of the most important features of the Ionic world of the period is the rise of strong personalities: in the political realm these are the Tyrants, in the poetic field we find the great elegiacs (Mimnermus), jambic poets (Hipponax) and lyric ones (Anacreon), in the architectural field the exceptional architect becomes established (Theodorus and Rhoecus), finally in the art of sculpture the great master emerges (Endoeus).

As a matter of fact, a few of these outstanding personalities lived in the court of Polycrates on Samus: Theodorus, Rhoecus, Ibycus, Anacreon must have made the Samian intellectual experience of these decades truly remarkable. Thus the 'invention' of a new literary genre meant to explain the new marvel – the dipterus – expresses the acquisition on the part of the prominent architect of the status of *artifex doctus*.

---

[4]H. Kienast, 'Die Dipteroi im Heraion von Samos', T. Schulz (ed.), *Dipteros und Pseudodipteros*, Duesseldorf (2012) 5-17.
[5]H. Svenson – Evers, *Die Griechischen Architekten archaischer und klassischer Zeit*, Frankfurt (1996) 7-49.
[6]Kienast (note 4).
[7]H. Kyrieleis, 'The Heraion at Samos', N. Marinatos and R. Haegg (ed.), *Greek Sanctuaries*, London (1993) 125-153.

It is very difficult to admit that the various features of the dipterus as well as this enormous decorative display could be described only by words: thus it is possible that illustrating drawings complemented the text and made it more understandable.

The Samian dipterus was soon imitated by the Ephesians who set up another colossal Ionic dipterus to their own goddess, the Ephesian Artemis.[8] The architects of the new, imposing, building, Chersiphron of Cnossus and his son Metagenes,[9] also imitated Theodorus and wrote a treatise about the Artemisium promoted by Croesus (the so-called 'Croesus'-Temple).

A summary of a section of this treatise is handed down by the same Vitruvius 10. 2. 11-12:

11. Non est autem alienum etiam Chersiphronos ingeniosam rationem exponere. is enim scapos columnarum e lapidicinis cum deportare vellet Ephesi ad Dianae fanum, propter magnitudinem onerum et viarum campestrem mollitudinem non confisus carris ne rotae devorarentur sic est conatus. de materia trientali scapos quattuor, duos transversarios interpositos, quanta longitudo scapi fuerat complectit et compegit et ferreos cnodacas uti subscudes in capitibus scaporum inplumbavit et armillas in materia ad cnodacas circumdandos infixit, item bucculis ligneis capita religavit. cnodaces autem in armillis inclusi liberam habuerant versationem tantam uti cum boves ducerent subiuncti, scapi versando in cnodacibus et armillis sine fine volverentur.

12. cum autem scapos omnes ita vexerant et instabant epistyliorum vecturae, filius Chersiphronos Metagenes transtulit <idem> e scaporum vectura etiam in epistyliorum deductione. fecit enim rotas circiter pedum duodenum et epistyliorum capita in medias rotas inclusit. eadem ratione cnodacas et armillas in capitibus inclusit. ita cum trientes a bubus ducerentur, in armillis inclusi cnodaces versabant rotas, epistylia vero inclusa uti axes in rotis eadem ratione qua scapi sine mora ad opus pervenerunt. exemplar autem erit eius quemadmodum in palaestris cylindri exaequant ambulationes. neque hoc potuisset fieri nisi primum propinquitas esset. non enim plus sunt ab lapidicinis ad fanum milia pedum octo, nec ullus est clivus sed perpetuus campus.[10]

'11. It is quite germane to our subject to describe an ingenious contrivance of Chersiphron. When he desired to bring down the shafts of the columns from the quarries to the Temple of Diana at Ephesus, he tried the following arrangement.

---

[8] About the archaic Ionic dipterus Artemisium, see A. Ohnesorg, 'Die beiden Dipteroi der Artemis von Ephesos', Schulz (note 4) 19-40.
[9] See Svenson – Evers (note 5) 67-99; R. Vollkommer, 'Chersiphron', Vollkommer (note 3) 1 (2001) 139 and A. Bammer, 'Metagenes', *ibidem* 2 (2004) 78-79.
[10] See Gros (note 2) 1310-1313.

1. THE TREATISES WRITTEN BY ARCHITECTS ABOUT SPECIFIC ARCHITECTURAL WORKS MADE BY THEM

For he distrusted his two-wheeled carts, fearing lest the wheels should sink down in the yielding country lanes because of the huge loads. He framed together four wooden pieces of four-inch timbers: two of them being cross-pieces as long as the stone column. At each end of the column, he ran in iron pivots with lead, dovetailing them, and fixed sockets in the wood frame to receive the pivots, binding the ends with wood cheeks: thus the pivots fitted into the sockets and turned freely. Thus when oxen were yoked and drew the frame, the columns turned in the sockets with their pivots and revolved without hindrance.

12. Now when they had thus brought all the shafts, and set about bringing the architraves, Metagenes, the son of Chersiphron, applied the method of conveying the shafts to the transport of the lintels. For he made wheels about twelve feet in diameter, and fixed the ends of the architraves in the middle of the wheels. In the same way he fixed pivots and sockets at the ends of the architraves. Thus when the frames of four-inch timber were drawn by the oxen, the pivots moving in the sockets turned the wheels, while the architraves being enclosed like axles in the wheels (in the same way as the shafts) reached the building without delay. (A similar machine is used when rollers level the walks in the palaestrae.) This expedient would not have been possible unless, to begin with, the distance had been short. It is not more than eight miles from the quarries to the temple, and there are no hills but an unbroken plain.' (transl. Loeb)

Pliny 36. 95-97 also appears to have used this treatise:

95
Graecae magnificentiae vera admiratio exstat templum Ephesiae Dianae CXX annis factum a tota Asia. in solo id palustri fecere, ne terrae motus sentiret aut hiatus timeret rursus ne in lubrico atque instabili fundamenta tantae molis locarentur, calcatis ea substravere carbonibus, dein velleribus lanae. universo templo longitudo est CCCCXXV pedum, latitudo CCXXV, columnae CXXVII a singulis regibus factae LX pedum altitudine, ex iis XXXVI caelatae, una a Scopa. operi praefuit Chersiphron architectus.

96
summa miraculi epistylia tantae molis attolli potuisse; id consecutus ille est aeronibus harenae plenis, molli clivo super capita columnarum exaggerato, paulatim exinaniens imos, ut sensim opus in loco sederet. difficillime hoc contigit in limine ipso, quod foribus inponebat; etenim ea maxima moles fuit nec sedit in cubili, anxio artifice mortis destinatione suprema.

97
tradunt in ea cogitatione fessum nocturno tempore in quiete vidisse praesentem deam, cui templum fieret, hortantem, ut viveret: se composuisse lapidem. atque ita postera luce apparuit; pondere ipso correctus videbatur. cetera eius operis ornamenta plurium librorum instar optinent, nihil ad specimen naturae pertinentia.[11]

---

[11] See A. Corso, R. Mugellesi, G. Rosati, Gaio Plinio Secondo Storia Naturale V, Turin (1988) 651-655.

'95. Of grandeur as conceived by the Greeks a real and remarkable example still survives, namely the temple of Diana at Ephesus, the building of it occupied all Asia for 120 years. It was built on marshy soil so that it might not be subject to earthquakes or be threatened by subsidences. On the other hand, to ensure that the foundations of so massive a building would not be laid on shifting, unstable ground, they were underpinned with a layer of closely trodden charcoal, and then with another of sheepskins with their fleeces unshorn. The length of the temple overall is 425 feet, and its breadth 225 feet. There are 127 columns, each constructed by a different king and 60 feet in height. Of these, 36 were carved with reliefs, one of them by Scopas. The architect in charge of the work was Chersiphron.

96. The crowning marvel was his success in lifting the architraves of this massive building into place. This he achieved by filling bags of plaited reed with sand and constructing a gently graded ramp which reached the upper surfaces of the capitals of the columns. Then, little by little, he emptied the lowest layer of bags, so that the fabric gradually settled into its right position. But the greatest difficulty was encountered with the lintel itself when he was trying to place it over the door; for this was the largest block, and it would not settle on its bed. The architect was in anguish as he debated whether suicide should be his final decision.

97. The story goes that in the course of his reflections he became weary, and that while he slept at night he saw before him the goddess for whom the temple was being built: she was urging him to live because, as she said, she herself had laid the stone. And on the next day this was seen to be the case. The stone appeared to have been adjusted merely by dint of its own weight. The other embellishments of the building are enough to fill many volumes, since they are in no way related to natural forms.' (transl. Loeb)

The technicalities invented by Chersiphron in order to bring columns and architraves to the site where the temple would have been set up are hardly clear only on the basis of a written text. Thus even in this case it is not unlikely that explanatory drawings were included in the volume, expressed the creativity of the architects and suggested the interpretation of their works as marvels.

During the central decades of the 5th c. BC, the habit by artists of writing treatises which explain their own oeuvre moved to Athens: that is understandable because at the time this *polis* certainly was the most creative and lively center in the Greek world.

Thus Agatharchus wrote a pamphlet about the scenery prepared by him for a tragedy by Aeschylus:[12] even in this case the rules about design, illustrated by Vitruvius below, and again in section 11, were hardly understandable without images.

---

[12] About Agatarco, G. Broeker and W. Mueller, 'Agatharchos (I)', Vollkommer (note 3) 1 (2001) 9

1. THE TREATISES WRITTEN BY ARCHITECTS ABOUT SPECIFIC ARCHITECTURAL WORKS MADE BY THEM

Perhaps the treatises of Democritus[13] and Anaxagoras[14] about the project may not have been complemented with images because they were more philosophical than theoretical.

The famous Ictinus[15] and his probable collaborator Carpion[16] wrote a treatise about the Parthenon. Vitruvius probably uses this treatise in 5. 1. 3:

Columnae superiores quarta parte minores quam inferiores sunt constituendae, propterea quod oneri ferendo quae sunt inferiora firmiora debent esse quam superiora, non minus quod etiam nascentium oportet imitari naturam, ut in arboribus teretibus, abiete cupressu pinu, e quibus nulla non crassior est ab radicibus, deinde crescendo proceditur in altitudinem naturali contractura peraequata nascens ad cacumen. Ergo si natura nascentium ita postulat, recte est constitutum et altitudinibus et crassitudinibus superiora inferiorum fieri contractiora.[17]

'The upper columns are to be a quarter less than the lower ones; because the lower columns ought to be stronger for bearing weight than the upper ones. Not less one ought also to imitate the natural growth of trees, as in tapering trees, the fir, the cypress, the pine, of which everyone is thicker at the roots. Then diminishing it rises on high, by a natural contraction growing evenly to the summit. Therefore since the nature of growing plants so demands, things are rightly arranged both in height and thickness, if the higher are more contracted than the lower.' (transl. Loeb)

In fact these prescriptions were applied in the double columnade of the eastern cella of the Parthenon. Moreover the mimetic theory implied by these remommendations is in keeping with the mimetic concept of figurative arts which it typical of classical Greece.

The Parthenon was characterized by a rich display of subtilities. In particular, the curvature of horizontal and vertical lines of the temple could hardly be explained only by words.[18] Thus even in this case the need for clarity may have required complementary drawings which would have accompanied the written text.

---

[13] See I. Bodnar, 'Demokritos', *DNP* 3 (1997) 455-458.
[14] See C. Pietsch, 'Anaxagoras (2)', *DNP* 1 (1996) 667-668.
[15] About Ictinus, see M. Korres, 'Iktinos', Vollkommer (note 3) 1 (2001) 338-345.
[16] About Carpion, M. Korres, 'Karpion', Vollkommer (note 3) 404-405. It is possible that treatises as that on the Parthenon are to be included among the syggraphai required by the state's patronage to the architects, as it is argued by Attic inscriptions of late classical period: evidence in G. Marginesu, 'Le 'azioni' degli architetti nell'Attica classica ed ellenistica', RA 2015. 1. 3-22, particularly 8.
[17] Gros (note 10) 553.
[18] About the mathematic genesis of the configurations of the Parthenon, the bibliography is huge. Here I cite only R. Brigo, 'Parthenon', Babesch 87 (2012) 159-17 and S. Borghini, 'Alexemata', F. Cantatore *et alii* (ed.), *Giornata di studio in onore di Claudio Tiberi, Rome* (2012) 27-38.

The publication of books about architecture or related fields appears to have become topical for the post-Periclean period: Vitruvius (section 14) lists a series of artists who wrote *praecepta symmetriarum*, about modular relations. The absence in this list of Polycleitus, who wrote a much praised 'Kanon',[19] is striking. However, the Greek formal experience which became the standard according to Vitruvius was that of the period between Pytheus and Hermogenes.

The first classical period was not lavished by this Hellenistic architect with the unconditional admiration it had enjoyed in Augustan times.

Having clarified the possible reason of the absence of Polycleitus in the Vitruvian catalogue of writers about *symmetriae*, it is time to consider, one by one, the writers who are included in the list:

1. *Nexaris*, totally unknown.
2. *Theocydes*, perhaps to be identified with the person from Delus who in the 370s was benefactor of the sanctuary of Apollo on this island:[20] in fact a close link with the god of measure is appropriate to a specialist in *symmetriae*.
3. *Demophilus*, perhaps the homonymous painter master of Zeuxis (Pliny 35. 61),[21] whose teaching would be at the basis of Zeuxis' interest in the modularity.
4. *Pollis*, probably the homonymous bronze sculptor of athletes, warriors, hunters and sacrificers (Pliny 34. 91).[22]
5. *Leonidas*, identified either with the homonymous painter student of Euphranor,[23] or with the homonymous architect of Naxus who built the *Leonidaion* at Olympia.[24]
6. *Silanion*, well known Athenian bronze sculptor of the late classical period, close to Plato.[25]
7. *Melampus*, perhaps the homonymous writer who lived in the court of the Ptolemaeans and wrote treatises about biting and the human body[26] because he was interested in rhythmical structures.
8. *Sarnacus*, otherwise unknown.
9. Finally Euphranor, renowned painter and bronze sculptor,[27] whose *volumina de symmetria et coloribus* were known to Pliny 35. 129.

---

[19] About the 'Kanon' of Polycleitus, see e. g. A. Stewart, 'Nuggets', *AJA* 102 (1998) 271-292.
[20] See J. S. Traill, *Persons of ancient Athens* 9, Toronto (2000) 177-178, nos.. 508483 and 508505.
[21] See R. Vollkommer, 'Demophilos (i) (ii)', Vollkommer (note 3) 1 (2001) 167.
[22] R. Vollkommer, 'Pollis (i)', Vollkommer (note 3) 2 (2004) 269 and W. Mueller, 'Pollis (ii)', *ibidem*.
[23] See R. Vollkommer, 'Leonidas (i)', Vollkommer (note 3) 2 (2004) 12.
[24] W. Mueller, 'Leonidas (ii)', Vollkommer (note 3) 2 (2004) 12-13. Although both these Leonidas lived in the late 4th c. BC, they cannot be the same person because they have different patronymics.
[25] M. Weber, 'Silanion', Vollkommer (note 3) 2 (2004) 385-386.
[26] H. Raeder, 'Melampus 6', *RE* 15. 1 (1931) 399.
[27] W. Mueller, 'Euphranor', Vollkommer (note 3) 1 (2001) 229-230.

1. THE TREATISES WRITTEN BY ARCHITECTS ABOUT SPECIFIC ARCHITECTURAL WORKS MADE BY THEM

Most of the artist-writers remembered by Vitruvius in this passage pertain to the late classical times: thus this period must have been a moment of frequent concern for the problem of modular relations in architecture as well as in painting and bronze sculpture.

It is possible that at least the specialists who wrote *ex professo* about architecture integrated their expositions with illustrations, which often were necessary for the sake of clarity.

Vitruvius also records treatises specifically about architecture which are pertinent to the late classical period as well. These books were either 'theoretical' treatises or *volumina* concerning specific buildings.

He mentions the following treatises of this type:

 a. The treatise by Theodorus of Phocaea about the *tholos* of Delphi.[28]
 b. The book of Pytheus about the temple of Athena at Priene.[29]
 c. The exposition of Satyrus and Pytheus about the Mausoleum.[30]
 d. The treatise of Arcesius about the Ionic temple of Asclepius at Tralles.
 e. The commentary of Philon about the arsenal of the Piraeus.[31]

The theoretic treatises of architecture are a little bit later than these treatises concerning specific monuments and probably were indebted to the Aristotelean habit of giving systematic presentations of the various branches of learning.

Thus Philon wrote *de aedium sacrarum symmetriis*.

Arcesius wrote *de symmetriis Corinthiis* where he probably gave the prescriptions about the Corinthian order collected by Vitruvius and which are appropriate to a phase of the Corinthian order around 350-330 BC.

Finally, *Silenus de symmetriis doricorum edidit volumen*. If the proportions suggested for the Doric order by this treatise are those prescribed by Vitruvius for the Doric temple, this book should date to the early Hellenistic period.

The period from the late 4th century BC to the 2nd sees an abrupt increase of technical treatises about machines. Vitruvius in section 14 of his introduction to book 7 lists 12 writers of *machinatio*. These treatises had been used by Vitruvius as he specifies in the same section 14. The explanations kept in these books

---

[28] W. Hoepfner, 'Zur Tholos in Delphi', *AA* (2000) 99-107.
[29] W. Koenigs, 'The Temple of Athena Polias at Priene', L. Haselberger (ed.), *Appearance and Essence*, Philadelphia (1999) 139-153.
[30] W. Hoepfner, *Halikarnassos und das Maussoleion*, Mainz (2013).
[31] E. Lorenzen, *The Arsenal at Piraeus*, Copenhagen (1964).

about the composition and working of these machines, which often were rather complicated, would have been rather difficult without illustrations.[32]

In the late 3rd century BC, Hermogenes wrote his two treatises about the pseudodipteros Ionic temple of Artemis at Magnesia[33] as well as about the monopterus of Dionysus at Theus.[34]

The immediate antecedents of the Vitruvian treatise are three works in Latin:

   a. The architectural treatise of Fuficius.[35]
   b. The *de architectura* by Varro[36] and
   c. The two books on the topic by Publius Settimius.[37]

Since Vitruvius mentions illustrations attached to his text, it is likely that he followed a habit established by his Latin predecessors, who thus may also have placed illustrations in their treatises.

---

[32] See about this issue M. Galli and G.. Pisani Sartorio (ed.), *Machina*, Rome (2009).
[33] B. Schmalz, ' "Aspectus" und "Effectus", Hermogenes und Vitruv', *RM* 102 (1996) 133-140.
[34] M. Uysal, *The Temple of Dionysos at Teos*, Izmir (1991).
[35] About the Fuficii, see G. Susini, 'Fundus Fangonianus', *Studi Romagnoli* 20 (1969) 333-339.
[36] See G. Moretti, Il manuale e l'allegoria', M. S. Celentano (ed.), *Ars / techne*, Alessandria (2003).
[37] See J. Bartels, 'Septimius I 5', *DNP* 11 (2001) 430.

2. The illustrations which accompanied the text of the *de architectura* by Vitruvius

Now it is time to take into consideration the passages of the treatise of Vitruvius in which drawings clarifying his text are mentioned. Although these illustrations are not found in the manuscript tradition, nevertheless their mentions in the *de architectura* provide important information about the field of architectural drawings in antiquity.

In 1. 1. 3, Vitruvius asserts that the architect with a complete expertise must be *peritus graphidos*, 'a skilful draughtsman'.

In 1. 1. 4, he specifies that the architect must know the *graphidos scientiam…, quo facilius exemplaribus pictis quam velit operis speciem deformare valeat*, 'by his skill in draughtsmanship he will find it easy by coloured drawings to represent the effect desired' (transl. Loeb).

In 1. 1. 13 he specifies that the architect, although he cannot be a painter of the quality of Apelles, nevertheless must be *graphidos non inperitus,* 'not unskilled with his pencil' (transl. Loeb).

Then, in 1. 2. 2 he illustrates the *ichnographia*, the drawing of the plan of a building, the *orthographia*, the drawing of the elevation of a building, and the *scaenographia*, the drawing of a building according to the rules of perspective.

In keeping with these theoretical assertions about the importance of drawings, Vitruvius in several cases refers to drawings attached to his text, which were often short and not very analytical and thus may have been not entirely understandable.

The first case of drawings cited by Vitruvius occurs in 1. 6. 12, a passage in which he introduces two drawings which illustrate the relations between the roads of a city and the blowing of the wind:

Quoniam haec a nobis sunt breviter exposita, ut facilius intellegantur visum est mihi in extremo volumine formas, sive uti Graeci σχηματα dicunt, duo explicare, unum ita deformatum ut appareat unde certi ventorum spiritus oriantur, alterum quemadmodum ab impetu eorum aversis directionibus vicorum et platearum evitentur nocentes flatus.[38]

---
[38] See Gros (note 2) 53-55.

'Since these matters have been briefly set forth by us, in order that it may be more easily understood I have decided at the end of the book to furnish two plans, or as the Greeks say *schemata:* one so mapped out that it may appear whence the certain breezes of the winds arise; the second, how by layings out of quarters and streets turned away from their violence, dangerous currents may be avoided.' (transl. Loeb)

Thus Vitruvius first of all gives the words which are used for these drawings *schemata* in Greek, *formae* in Latin. The two drawings shown were found at the end of the book. The first of them was a sort of rose of winds, the second offered a network of roads of a city with orientations designed to avoid winds that blew dangerously.

The authour thus teaches (1. 6. 12-13) how these drawings have to be prepared and how they work:

Erit autem in exaequata planitie centrum ubi est littera A, gnomonis autem antemeridiana umbra ubi est B, et a centro ubi est A diducto circino ad id signum umbrae ubi est B, circumagatur linea rotundationis. reposito autem gnomone ubi antea fuerat, expectanda est dum decrescat faciatque iterum crescendo parem antemeridianae umbrae postmeridianam tangatque lineam rotundationis ubi erit littera C. tunc a signo ubi est B et a signo ubi est C circino decussatim describatur ubi erit D, deinde per decussationem ubi est D et centrum perducatur linea ad extremum, in qua linea erunt litterae E et F. haec linea erit index meridianae et septentrionalis regionis.

13. tunc circino totius rotundationis sumenda est pars XVI, circinique centrum ponendum est in meridiana linea qua tangit rotundationem ubi est littera E, et signandum dextra ac sinistra ubi erunt litterae G et H. Item in septentrionali parte centrum circini ponendum in rotundatione et septentrionali linea ubi est littera F, et signandum dextra ac sinistra ubi sunt litterae I et K, et ab G ad K et ab H ad I per centrum lineae perducendae. ita quod erit spatium ab G ad H, erit spatium venti austri et partis meridianae, item quod erit spatium ab I ad K, erit septentrionis. reliquae partes dextra tres ac sinistra tres dividendae sunt aequaliter, quae sunt ad orientem in quibus litterae L M et ab occidente in quibus sunt litterae N et O. ab M ad O et ab L ad N perducendae sunt lineae decussatim. et ita erunt aequaliter ventorum octo spatia in circumitione. quae cum ita descripta erunt, in singulis angulis octagoni cum a meridie incipiemus inter eurum et austrum in angulo erit littera G, inter austrum et africum H, inter africum et favonium N, inter favonium et caurum O, inter caurum et septentrionem K, inter septentrionem et aquilonem I, inter aquilonem et solanum L, inter solanum et eurum M. ita his confectis inter angulos octagoni gnomon ponatur, et ita dirigantur angiportorum divisiones.'[39]

---

[39] Gros (note 2) 55.

2. THE ILLUSTRATIONS WHICH ACCOMPANIED THE TEXT OF THE *DE ARCHITECTURA* BY VITRUVIUS

'Now there shall be on a levelled surface a centre with the letter A; the shadow before midday of the indicator, with B; and from the centre marked A the compass is opened to the point of shadow marked B, and a circle is to be drawn. The indicator being replaced where it was before, we must wait until the shadow diminishes, and again by increasing makes the shadow after midday equal to that before midday and touches the circle at the letter C. Then from B and from C let the intersection D be described with the compasses; then through the intersection D and the centre, let a line be carried through to the furthest limit, where will be the letter E and also F, and on this line will be the index of the southern and northern regions.

13. Then the sixteenth part of the whole circle is to be taken with the compass, and the point of the compass is to be put on the meridian line where it touches the circumference at E, and a mark is to be made right and left at GH. Also in the northern part, the point of the compass is to be placed on the circumference and the northern line where is the letter F, and a mark is to be made right and left at I and K. And from G and K and from H to I, lines are to be drawn through the centre. So the space from G to H will be the space of the Auster and of the southern region; likewise the space from I to K will be of the Septentrio. The remaining parts, on the right three, and the left three, are to be divided equally; those which are to the east at L and M, and at the west at N and O. From M to O and from L to N intersecting lines are to be drawn. And so there will be eighth equal spaces of winds in the circumference. When these are so marked out, at the single angles of the octagon when we begin from the south, in the angle between Eurus and Auster there will be G, between Auster and Africus there will be H, between Africus and Favonius N, between Favonius and Caurus O, between Caurus and Septentrio K, between Septentrio and Aquilo I, between Aquilo and Solanus L, between Solanus and Eurus M. When these things are done, let the gnomon be set upon the angles of the octagon and let the division of the alleys be directed accordingly (transl. Loeb).

In 2. *Praef.* 2 Dinocrates shows Alexander his projects (*formae*), whose high quality is understood by the Macedonian king (2. *Praef.* 3: *egregiae formae compositio*):

At ille, Dinocrates, inquit, architectus Macedo, qui ad te cogitationes et formas adfero dignas tuae claritatis. namque Athon montem formavi in statuae virilis figuram, cuius manu laeva designavi civitatis amplissimae moenia, dextra pateram quae exciperet omnium fluminum quae sunt in eo monte aquam, ut inde in mare profunderetur.

3. delectatus Alexander natione formae statim quaesiit, si essent agri circa qui possent frumentaria ratione eam civitatem tueri. cum invenisset non posse nisi transmarinis subvectionibus, Dinocrates, inquit, attendo egregiam formae compositionem et ea delector.[40]

'And he (*scil.*: Dinocrates) replied (*scil.*: to Alexander): 'Dinocrates, a Macedonian architect, who brings you ideas and plans worthy of you, illustrious prince. For I have shaped Mount Athos into the figure of the statue of a man, in whose left hand I have shown the ramparts of a very extensive city; in his right a bowl to receive the water of all the rivers which are in that mountain, so that this water falls down on the sea.'

3. Alexander, delighted with his kind of plan, at once inquired if there were fields about, which could furnish that city with a corn supply. When he found this could not be done, except by sea transport, he said: 'I note, Dinocrates, the unusual formation of your plan, and I am pleased with it'. (transl. Loeb with amendments)

This passage suggests a second function of the drawing: not only practical / illustrative, but also aesthetical, apt to provoke the *delectatio*. In fact Alexander is *delectatus* by this *forma*.

In 3 *praef.* 4 he remembers that:

ventique qui sint et e quibus singuli spirent deformationibus grammicis ostendi

'I (…) showed by geometrical figures the various winds, and the quarters from which they severally blow' (transl. Loeb).[41]

Of course he refers to both drawings of the first book, which thus are regarded crucial elements of this exposition.

In 3. 3. 13, he prefers not to explain with words how a perfect entasis can be done and to invite the readers to learn it from a drawing placed at the end of the book:

de adiectione quae adicitur in mediis columnis, quae apud Graecos ἔντασις appellatur, in extremo libro erit formata ratio eius quemadmodum mollis et conveniens efficiatur subscripta.

'As to the swelling which is made in the middle of the columns (this among the Greeks is called *entasis*), an illustrated formula will be furnished at the end of the

---
[40] Gros (note 2) 117.
[41] Gros (note 2) 237.

book to show how the entasis may be done in a graceful and appropriate manner' (transl. Loeb).[42]

In this specific case, there is no doubt that the difficulty to explain a rather complicated formula led the writer to the decision to refer to a *formata ratio*.

Because of the same need to avoid a complicated and obscure explanation, Vitruvius does not specify by words how to curve the horizontal lines of the temple through the *scamilli inpares* but refers to a drawing placed at the end of the book (3. 4. 5):

hoc autem ut scamilli ad id convenientes fiant, item in extremo libro forma et demonstratio erit descripta.

'The method of making the risers suitable to this will be set out with a figure and demonstration at the end of the book' (transl. Loeb).[43]

This specification clarifies that the visual component of these plates (*forma*) was complemented with captions (*demonstratio*).

For the sake of clarity, Vitruvius provides a drawing with explanations as to how to obtain a good Ionic volute, which he also describes with words, but without important details (3. 5. 8):

de volutarum descriptionibus, uti ad circinum sint recte involutae quemadmodum describantur, in extremo libro forma et ratio earum erit subscripta.

'At the end of the book a diagram and formula will be furnished for the drawing of the volutes so that they may be correctly turned by the compass' (transl. Loeb).[44]

In 3. 5. 14 he refers to the previously mentioned drawing of the entasis because it provides the width of the flutes:

crassitudines striarum faciendae sunt quantum adiectio in media columna ex descriptione invenietur.

'The width of the flutes must correspond to the swelling in the middle of the column which is argued by its description'.[45]

---

[42] Gros (note 2) 251.
[43] Gros (note 2) 255.
[44] Gros (note 2) 259.
[45] Gros (note 2) 261.

In the fourth book, the writer refers again to the plate of the third book about the entasis, in the context of his perameters concerning Doric columns (4. 3. 10):

de adiectione eius quae media adaugetur, uti in tertio volumine de ionicis est perscripta, ita et in his transferatur.

'Concerning the entasis of the column by which it is increased in the middle, the method prescribed in the third book for the Ionic order is to be imitated in the case of the Doric order' (transl. Loeb).[46]

In 4. 8. 7 the writer refers to the difficulty of explaining his matter with words: *quoad potui significare scriptis exposui,* 'as far as I could indicate by writing'.[47] The difficulty of explaining only with text of course is the reason why plates have been adopted in this treatise.

In 4. 9. 1 he refers to the *ararum deformationes, i. e.* to the drawings of altars. This specification stresses the importance of drawings in the architectural practice conceived by our architect: drawings are instrumental both to the learning of the *ars* as well as to the creation of the project.

In the fifth book, in the explanation concerning the *echeia*, Vitruvius refers to another plate at the end of this book which reproduced the diagram of Aristoxenus (5. 4. 1 and 5. 6): itaque ut potuero quam apertissime ex Aristoxenis scripturis interpretabor et eius diagramma subscribam finitionesque sonituum designabo, uti qui diligentius attenderit facilius percipere possit.

(…)

haec autem si qui voluerit ad perfectum facile perducere, animadvertat in extremo libro diagramma musica ratione designatum, quod Aristoxenus magno vigore et industria generatim divisis modulationibus constitutum reliquit. de quo si qui ratiocinationibus his attenderit, ad naturas vocis et audientium delectationes facilius valuerit theatrorum efficere perfectiones.

'Therefore, I shall translate (as well as I can) from the works of Aristoxenus subjoining his diagram, and I shall indicate the definitions of the musical notes, so that an attentive reader can the more easily understand' (transl. Loeb).[48]

(…)

---

[46] Gros (note 2) 385.
[47] Gros (note 2) 397.
[48] Gros (note 2) 561.

2. THE ILLUSTRATIONS WHICH ACCOMPANIED THE TEXT OF THE *DE ARCHITECTURA* BY VITRUVIUS

'If anyone wishes to bring all this to execution, let him note at the end of the book a diagram drawn in accordance with the method of music, which Aristoxenus, employing a sound and careful method, has left us arranged with the modulations according to their kinds. If he attends to these calculations, he will the more easily be able to erect theatres adapted to the nature of the voice and the pleasure of the audience' (transl. Loeb).[49]

In this case, this plate is justified by the need of placing the *echeia* in their appropriate places in theatres, which is stressed by Vitruvius.

Still in the fifth book (5. 9. 4), he refers to the plate of the third book concerning the *scamilli inpares* for the curvature of the horizontal lines of porticoes:

stylobatisque adiectio quae fit per scamillos inpares, ex descriptione quae supra scripta est in libro tertio sumatur.

'The addition to the stylobates is to be made by unequal ordinates in accordance with the description which is given above in the third book' (transl. Loeb).[50]

The sixth book had no plates but in 6. 1. 7 the musical diagram of the previous book is mentioned:

igitur quae nationes sunt inter axis meridiani cardinem ab septentrionalis medio positae, uti in diagrammate musico medianae vocis habent sonitum in sermone.

'Therefore the nations which are placed in the middle between the equator and the north pole have in conversation a middle accent corresponding to the musical diagram' (transl. Loeb).[51]

The absence of plates also characterizes the seventh book.

In the eighth book, Vitruvius in his chapter about the chorobates (8. 5. 3), refers to a drawing at the end of the book:

exemplar autem chorobati erit in extremo volumine descriptum.

'A drawing of the chorobates is furnished at the end of the book' (transl. Loeb).[52]

In the ninth book, two figures were displayed at the bottom of the related pages and not at the end of the book.

---
[49] Gros (note 2) 567.
[50] Gros (note 2) 579.
[51] Gros (note 2) 831.
[52] Gros (note 2) 1139.

The first of these two plates was the *schema* of the duplication of the square in 9. *Praef.* 5:

hac ratione duplicatio grammicis rationibus ab Platone, uti schema subscriptum est in ima pagina, explicata est.

'In this manner the duplication is demonstrated geometrically by Plato in accordance with the figure subjoined at the bottom of the page'(transl. Loeb).[53]

The second plate of the ninth book showed the positioning of ladders with indication of the levels of steps (9. *Praef.* 8):

item eius rei erit subscripta forma.

'The drawing of this, also, is subjoined' (transl. Loeb).[54]

Finally in the tenth book, Vitruvius in 10. 6. 4 refers to a plate placed in the end of the book that illustrates the screw of Archimedes:

qua ratione autem oporteat id esse, in extremo libro eius forma descripta est in ipso tempore.

'How this is to be done is shown by a diagram at the end of the book' (transl. Loeb).[55]

Summing up, Vitruvius in his *de architectura* mentions 10 drawings: eight of them were placed at the end of books, while two of them, illustrating the *praefatio* to the ninth book, had been placed at the bottom of pages.

The reason of this choice probably stems from the circumstance that the two drawings of the ninth book are the only ones illustrating an introduction and thus may have been regarded as independent from the context of the related book.

The book which had most drawings was the third, which had three plates: this is due to the circumstances, that Vitruvius explains in this book, including issues such as the entasis, the curvatures of the horizontal lines of a temple and the Ionic volute, which could hardly be explained with words.

The first book and the ninth one had each one two drawings: the first book is on the rose of winds and on the orientation of roads, while the ninth book was endowed with two plates on the duplication of the square and on the model

---

[53] Gros (note 2) 1201.
[54] Gros (note 2) 1203.
[55] Gros (note 2) 1325.

2. THE ILLUSTRATIONS WHICH ACCOMPANIED THE TEXT OF THE *DE ARCHITECTURA* BY VITRUVIUS

of ladders with the levels of steps. The two drawings of the first book may have responded to the need for clarity, while those of the ninth book are not closely related to the matter considered in this book and thus probably respond to the wish of the writer to impress his readers.

Finally the books fifth, eighth and tenth had each one illustration. The fifth book had the diagram for the display of the *echeia* in theatres. This drawing responded to the need for clarity, because the use of *echeia* was unknown in Rome. The eighth book was endowed with a drawing on the chorobates. This was an instrument for the levelling of routes for water, which could hardly be explained only with words, without a visual representation of the object. Finally the tenth book was endowed with a drawing of the screw of Archimedes, which was also a complicated instrument, whose verbal explanation was not easy.

Thus it was the need to explain clearly these matters which led Vitruvius to the decision to attach drawings to his treatise. Moreover the anecdote of Alexander *delectatus* by a drawing project of Dinocrates suggests also that the aesthetic reason – the aim of making his treatise attractive – also contributed to the decision by Vitruvius to provide illustrations.

Of course his decision to endow his treatise with plates was also indebted to a long tradition In fact the consideration of the drawing as a dignifying addition and preliminary guarantee of the high quality of a final product had been already asserted by Parrhasius,[56] and after him by the school of Sicyon,[57] and thus became common sense in the world of the *videndae artes* in the following periods.

In the architectural field, drawings often were composed in construction yards prior to actual building work, in order to guarantee its exactness and adherence to established modular criteria. This practice is known by several documents, the most important of which are constituted by the many drawings incised on walls of the internal courtyard as well as on a wall of the *pronaos* of the temple of Apollo Philesios at Didyma, which date to the central decades of the 3rd century BC (see below). Among these drawings, there is an example on the socle of the north wall of the *adyton* which represents the entasis of a column and thus corresponds to the subject of a plate of Vitruvius: that mentioned in 3. 3. 13 , in 3. 5. 14 and in 4. 3. 10 which explained how an entasis was made. This coincidence suggested to Haselberger two hypotheses[58]: 1. that Vitruvius depended on drawings made in construction yards for his plates, such as those evidenced at Didyma; and 2. that in any case he follows the tradition of the Ionian temple architecture of Asia Minor from the early Hellenistic period.

---

[56] Pliny 35. 67.
[57] Pliny 35. 76.
[58] See L. Haselberger, 'Old Issues, new research, later discoveries', L. Haselberger (ed.), *Appearance and Essence*, Philadelphia (1999) 1-68.

This opinion is in keeping with the well known dependence of many Vitruvian directions from writings and monuments of the Ionic world of the period from Pytheus to Hermogenes, which has often been underlined by scholars of Vitruvius.[59]

However there is another possibility: that both drawings in construction yards and plates in the *de architectura* descend from treatises on specific, important architectural enterprises published by their architects in the Greek world, especially in the Ionic one, ranging from the height of development in the archaic period until the early Hellenistic one (see above).

In fact the buildings explained in these treatises were endowed with features, such as the volutes of Ionic capitals and the entasis, which could hardly have been explained only with words. Moreover these treatises were often addressed to the political patrons of these monuments who probably had no specialized competence on very technical architectural issues. Finally Ictinus and Carpion may have felt the need in their treatise about the Parthenon to explain how the systematic curvatures of the horizontal lines of this temple had been obtained. Thus in those cases it is at least plausible that the written comment had been accompanied by drawings. These plates may have been updated when new architectural *miracula* were set up and the related commentaries were published. Vitruvius may have continued this tradition when he published a text on architecture enriched by plates.

Moreover even the widespread diffusion of illustrated books may have influenced the creation of the Vitruvian drawings. Although illustrated books may have already existed in the classical period,[60] this type of book became well rooted particularly during the 3rd and 2nd centuries BC, especially in important Hellenistic centres, endowed with rich libraries and a conspicuous publishing activity, such as Alexandria and Pergamum.[61]

Evidence from papyri suggests that scientific texts – of music, mathematics, astronomy, botanics, medicine, geography, etc. – were accompanied by illustrations, which were deemed necessary to the understanding of these matters, at least from the early Hellenistic times:[62] it is obvious that the phenomenon of scientific illustrations, once it became a well established tradition, would explain the illustrations of the books first, fifth, eighth, ninth and tenth of the *de*

---

[59] See A. Corso, 'I disegni che corredavano il de architectura', P. Clini (ed.), *Vitruvio e il disegno di architettura*, Venice (2012) 47-59 with previous bibliography .
[60] See *e. g.* H. Blanck, *Das Buch in der Antike*, Munich (1992) 102-112.
[61] See Settis (note 1) for lists of illustrated papyri with a scientific character.
[62] Evidence in A. Soldati, 'L'illustrazione libraria', C. Gallazzi e S. Settis (ed.), *Le tre vite del papiro di Artemidoro*, Turin (2006) 132-139.

2. THE ILLUSTRATIONS WHICH ACCOMPANIED THE TEXT OF THE *DE ARCHITECTURA* BY VITRUVIUS

architectura, which may have been taken from these books (see *e. g.* the clear statements by Vitruvius 5. 4. 1 and 5. 6 that the diagram attached to the end of the fifth book was taken from Aristoxenus, probably from the *de musica* of this intellectual from Tarentum).

In a moment and in a cultural environment closer to that of Vitruvius, we have to consider the personality of Varro. He systematically integrated texts and images in his *Hebdomades* o *Imagines*: the descriptions of important and historical figures were accompanied by portraits of the same persons. Varro, a great authority, may have imposed with his *Imagines* a model of integration between word and image because a few years later even Atticus composed a book with images of famous men captioned by epigrams concerning their accomplishments.[63]

The interest of Varro for this mix of written and visual may suggest that he endowed his book, *de architectura,* with plates in the context of his treatise *de novem disciplinis*.

In that case, the treatise by Varro would be the immediate precursor to Vitruvius not only for a lot of the information given in Vitruvius' *de architectura* but also for his presentation of illustrations.

---

[63] See Nepos, *Atticus* 18. 5-6 and Pliny 35. 12.

3. Drawings included in handbooks after Vitruvius

The value of the Vitruvian drawings during the Roman imperial period is beyond any doubt.

Pliny utilized Vitruvius a lot in his books 16, 35 and 36 [64] but he took information from the text of the *de architectura* and never refers to drawings attached to that treatise.

Frontinus, *De aquae ductu Urbis Romae* 1. 17. 3-4 specifies that he ordered the preparation of drawn plans (*formae*) of the aqueducts of Rome, however he took this decision in order to place these plans in his office and did not publish them in his own treatise.

However, since he remembers Vitruvius in 1. 25. 1-2, he may have had in mind previous examples of that architect when he decided to commission these drawings.

Probably during Severan times, Faventinus wrote the *Artis architectonicae privatis usibus adbreviatus liber*, a treatise whose content was largely taken from Vitruvius: however he does not refer to drawings included in the *de architectura* nor does he enrich his summary with drawings of his own.

The same should be said of the *Opus agriculturae* of Rutilius Taurus Aemilianus Palladius, probably dating from the middle of the 5th century: Vitruvius is a primary source of information for the chapters of this book devoted to the villa, to building materials, to types of walls as well as to the plastering.[65] Even in this case the reference is always and only to the text of Vitruvius, never to his plates. Of course Palladius did not furnish figures in his treatise because this practice was never adopted by the *scriptores rei rusticae*.

At the beginning of the 7th century, Isidorus of Sevilla uses Vitruvius first of all for his ambition to give a new synthesis to the architectural science (*Etimologiae sive Origines* 15: *de aedificiis et agris*), moreover for his distinction between public buildings (15. 2: *de aedificiis publicis*), private ones (15. 3: *de habitaculis*) and sacred ones (15. 4: *de aedificiis sacris*), for very detailed information.[66]

---

[64] See Pliny 1. 16; 35 and 36.
[65] See Palladius 1. 8-40; 6. 11-12 and 9. 8-12 and 15.
[66] For the distinction between Doric, Ionic, Tuscanic and Corinthian columns (15. 8. 13), for building materials (16. 1-3), for specific trees (17. 7), for the moments which compose the building process (19. 9-10) as well as for colours (19. 17).

3. Drawings included in handbooks after Vitruvius

However he never cites Vitruvian illustrations nor does he provides visual tools for his new encyclopedy.

This absence of interest toward the drawings of the *de architectura* requires an explanation. Probably this fact has to do with the decline during the middle and late Roman imperial period of the concept of architecture as a theoretical science based on projects following geometric-modular principles. This concept of architecture had enjoyed great prestige during the classical, Hellenistic and early Roman periods but was no longer prevalent. That change of perspective must have implied a loss of interest for drawings illustrating complicated operations such as curvature of the horizontal lines of a building, volutes of Ionic capitals, the entasis etc. These features were typical of a model of architecture which was no longer topical. From Martial (*De spectaculis* 1) to Ausonius (*Mosella* 287-340) and later, the great architecture of contemporary times were exalted much more than the temples of the past such as the Artemisium of Ephesus and the Parthenon.[67]

This current became particularly dominant in the age of the *ekphraseis* of the new ecclesiastic architecture, from Paulus Silentiarius to Venantius Fortunatus. Whoever loved these new marvels must have no longer nourished a great interest for the most ingenious features of 'ancient' temples.

We should also consider that in the period from around 550 to 750 in the Latin west the most learned scholars, from Venantius Fortunatus to Isidorus, from the Venerable Bede to Virgil of Tolosa, reveal a great interest for the pre-Christian Roman world, but cultivate especially the great literature of the past and are much less interested (with the partial exception of Isidorus) to the ancient visual heritage.

These considerations probably explain why the Vitruvian illustrations have not been handed down in the manuscript tradition of the *de architectura*. Their loss probably dates before the redaction of the Carolingian archetype of the surviving codes of the Vitruvian treatise.

---

[67] Evidence in A. Corso, 'L'anticlassicismo nel gusto e nella critica d'arte da Roma a Costantinopoli', *NumAntCl* 39 (2010) 425-446.

4. Images attached to ancient descriptions of architecture

Now it is time to consider the literary genre named 'ekphrasis': this word means 'description', thus it also designates literary descriptions. These descriptions may focus on nature, landscapes and human beings. However, from Homer onwards, worthy manufacts are also described in literary works.[68]

The first surviving example of a description of an important artefact is the lengthy consideration of the shield of Achilles in Homer, *Iliad* 18. vv. 479-608.[69] As far as the field of architecture is concerned, the representations on this shield included two cities, in one of which an agora and a circular court of justice appeared, while in the other town there were walls, shipfolds and a place for dances.

The *ekphrasis* of the shield of Achilles was imitated in a poem attributed to Hesiod – the *Scutum Herculis* – in which the shield of Heracles is analytically considered (vv. 139-320). The friezes on this shield included an agora, as well as a harbour, a city with walls, towers and gates, another city also with gates, and finally a hippodrome for racing carriages.

The ancient editions of Homer and Hesiod were not endowed with visual representations of these poetic descriptions[70]: no reference to plates attached to these *ekdoseis* is found in the ancient literature. Thus we must suppose that the audience of these poems were free to imagine how these shields looked like.

Descriptions of architecture are found also in surviving tragedies. A passage of the 'Ion' by Euripides (vv. 184-218) is particularly noteworthy: it describes the temple of Apollo at Delphi with its sculptural display.[71] Since the dramatic action is supposed to take place in front of this temple, it is logical to suppose that its representation was included in the painted background of the stage and it is at least possible that even the sculptures evoked in this *fabula* were visualized.

---

[68] About the *ekphrasis*, see F. Graf, 'Ekphrasis', G. Boehm (ed.), *Beschreibungskunst*, Munich (1995) 143-155; A. Zumbo, 'L'ekphrasis d'opera d'arte', E. A. Arslan (ed.), *La 'parola' delle immagini*, Messina (1998) 29-40 and R. Webb, *Ekphrasis*, Farnham (2009).
[69] Concerning the shield of Achilles, see M. D'Acunto and R. Palmisciano (ed.), *Lo scudo di Achille nell'Iliade*, Pisa (2010) and K. Johnson, 'Sequential Narrative and the Shield of Achilles', G. Kovacs and C. W. Marshall (ed.), *Classics and Comics*, Oxford (2011) 43-58.
[70] About the ancient *ekdoseis* of Homer, see H. van Thiel, *Aristarch, Aristophanes Byzantios, Demetrios, Ixion, Zenodot*, Berlin (2014). Concerning representations of Homeric passages in Roman times, see D. Petrain, *Homer in Stone*, Cambridge (2014).
[71] Concerning Euripides as source for the visual culture of the period, see M. C. Stieber, *Euripides and the Language of Craft*, Boston (2011). The description of the house of Ion with decorated carpets (Euripides, *Ion*, vv. 1132-1165) is also important: see G. R. B. Turner, 'Well-Rowed Ships', *The Ancient History Bulletin* 22 (2008) 33-52.

We should also consider the ekphrastic epigram: often these poems describe works of art.[72] The use of composing short poems in order to describe works of art becomes established in the second quarter of the 4th c. B. C. One of the pioneers of this habit is the same Plato who in a couple of epigrams (*Anthologia Graeca* 16. 160-161) describes the Cnidian Aphrodite, while in another short poem he evokes the sleeping Eros (*Anthologia Graeca* 16. 210). The driving patterns of the ekphrastic epigram are the expressions of the illusionistic power of the work of art as well as the sense of life which pervades this creation.

Moreover sometimes the artistic representation is regarded as even more impressive than the corresponding subject in nature.

The ekphrastic epigram reflects the growing social praise of the work of art itself, as well as of the artist.[73] However the ecphrastic epigram describes, in the field of the artefacts, in most cases sculptures, paintings or images broadly defined as in the so called 'minor arts'. Architecture is usually not categorized in this genre, as is obvious, because the main aims of these poems are the praise of the sense of life and of the movement of the described figures.

The fashion of writing descriptive poems also pervades the Hellenistic poetry, even outside epigrams.[74] This poetic production focuses on a few architectural examples: the most noteworthy of these is the long presentation about the palace of Aeetes in Colchis by Apollonius Rhodius, *Argonautics* 3, vv. 215-248. This digression is very detailed and based on the need to emulate images through a purely verbal *ekphrasis*. It goes without saying that the poet wanted to win this contest between word and image: thus the *ekphrasis* of this palace is supposed to be more impressive than any visual representation of the same subject could be.[75]

Moreover the descriptions of the pavilion and of the procession of Ptolemaeus II at Alexandria by Callixenus of Rhodes, of the yacht of Jeron II of Syracuse by Moschion and of the procession and pavilion of Antiochus IV of Syria at Daphne by Polybius were very detailed.[76] These monumental creations were all ephemeral and extremely lavish. The descriptions by these writers are so exhaustive that modern scholars attempted to depict with drawings what these luxury monuments looked like. Even in these cases, it is possible to find discrepancies between

---

[72] See I. Maennlein-Robert, 'Epigrams on Art', P. Brug (ed.), *Brill's Companion to Hellenistic Epigram*, Leiden (2007) 251-271.
[73] See P. Schultz, 'Style and Agency in an Age of Transition', R. Osborne (ed.), *Debating the Athenian Cultural Revolution*, Cambridge (2007) 144-187.
[74] The evidence about the *ekphraseis* of works of art in the Hellenistic poetry has been collected by F. Manakidou, *Beschreibung von Kunstwerken in der Hellenistischen Dichtung*, Stuttgart (1993).
[75] See Manakidou (note 74) 157-173.
[76] See E. Calandra, *The Ephemeral and the Eternal*, Athens (2011); E. E. Rice, *The Grand Procession of Ptolemy Philadelphus*, Oxford (1983); B. Pace, 'La nave di Gerone', *Atti Accademia Palermo* 12 (1921) 3-25 and J. G. Bunge, 'Die Feiern Antiochos' IV. Epiphanes in Daphne', *Chiron* 6 (1976) 53-71.

word and image: although the public can no longer see these ephemeral works, nevertheless the *logos* can describe them accurately, despite their complexity. It is possible that such analytic descriptions, which have no precedents in the surviving Greek literature, were already found in the essays on temples and other buildings written by their architects, which have been considered in the previous pages. In this case, descriptions of temples and other buildings exemplified the life of the *polis* would have been replaced by evocations of luxury objects which expressed the power of absolute rulers.

Thus detailed descriptions are not found in the surviving regional literature of the Hellenistic period, of which only fragments are known.[77] That is logical because this literary genre gave only cursory presentations of monuments, without lenghty descriptions of single monuments.

Another field explored by the ekphrastic literature of the middle and late Hellenistic period is the description of ruins. The epigrams on the desolation of Corinth's ruins after 146 B. C. (*Anthologia Graeca* 7. 297 and 493 and 9. 151 and 284) mark the beginning of the taste for ruins. The latter is due to the retrospective trend for classicism at that time, the admiration for a past regarded great and superior to the present, and finally to the rising fascination for the picturesque.[78]

In the Latin literature, the first surviving description of a building is that of the Olympieion of Agrigentum by Naevius in his *Bellum Poenicum*.[79]

The Hellenistic tradition of very detailed descriptions was continued in Rome by Varro in the *De re rustica* 3. 5. 8-17 where he describes the aviary in his villa at Casinum: this writer gives even the measures of the various components of this architectural complex, so far that reconstruction drawings of this aviary based on the description by Varro have been created by modern scholars.[80]

The same Varro described the labyrinth of Porsenna at Clusium (Varro in Pliny 36. 91-93), once again giving the measures of the main parts of the monument.[81]

Varro describes Italian marvels probably in order to oppose them to those advertised by Greek writers. The habit of providing measures of the described

---

[77] See M. Angelucci, 'Polemone di Ilio', *Studi Classici e Orientali* 49 (2003) 165-184. Moreover S. Bianchetti, 'Peripli e periegesi', *Hesperi'a* 30 (2013) 221-239.
[78] About the taste for ruins, M. Barbanera (a c. di), *Metamorfosi delle rovine*, Milano (2013).
[79] Naevius, *Bellum Poenicum*, *frgg.* 44-46 Warmington. See C. Marconi, 'Titani e Zeus Olimpio', *Prospettiva* 87 (1997) 2-13.
[80] See A. Cassatella, 'La voliera di Varrone a Cassino', G. Ghini (ed.), *Lazio e la Sabina* 3, Rome (2006) 333-340.
[81] See J. –R. Jannot, 'Encore la tombe de Porsenna', *MEFRA* 117 (2005) 2. 633-649.

works probably was meant to allow the reader to figure out exactly what the evoked *miracula* looked like.

During the Augustan period, the most important patterns of Hellenistic poetry, including *ekphraseis,* were emulated by the most important poets of the age, even if the functions of these descriptions had changed.

Thus Vergil, *Aeneid* 1, vv. 418-493 describes Carthage and particularly the local temple of Juno with its figurative display.

Propertius also describes the sanctuary of Apollo Palatinus with the temple and the other monuments erected there (2. 31, vv. 1-16).

The description by Vergil exalts the beginning of the *imperium*, whilst the description by Propertius focuses on the shining glory of his native Rome.

Propertius (4. 10, vv. 27-30) also indulges this taste for ruins and evokes the old and destroyed city of Veii: this description is indebted both to the reception of a Hellenistic tradition (see above), and also to the perception of time eating everything, which is typical of Augustan culture (see Horace, *Carmina* 1. 11 and Ovid, *Metamorphoses* 15. 234-236).

The early Imperial period saw the continuity of the tradition of describing important buildings, whose measurements are sometimes also reported, in analytic detail.

In the age of Domitian, Statius describes the villa of Vopiscus at Tibur (*Silvae* 1. 3), the baths of Claudius Etruscus (*Silvae* 1. 5) as well as the villa of Pollius Felix at Surrentum (*Silvae* 2. 2).[82] These poetic descriptions of lavish private architecture, made for leisure purposes, are evoked only in the literary realm, drawings of architecture are never mentioned.

The descriptions by Pliny the Elder of the Mausoleum of Halicarnassus (36. 30-31) and of the Artemisium of Ephesus (36. 95-97) are particularly noteworthy.

The most important examples of epigrams devoted to architecture are also from the Flavian period: including the *De spectaculis* by Martial for the inauguration of the Colosseum. These poems praise the social function of the Colosseum and juxtapose it to the old fashioned marvels of the Greek world.

---

[82] See B. M. Gauly, 'Das Glueck des Pollius Felix', *Hermes* 134 (2006) 455-470.

The nephew of Pliny the Elder, Pliny the Younger, also exercized in this literary genre and described in detail his two villas (Pliny the Younger, *Epistulae* 2. 17 and 5. 6).[83]

In the second of these two descriptions (section 13), the writer refers to a possible painted drawing of the highest possible beauty (*formam aliquam ad eximiam pulchritudinem pictam*), representing a hypothetic villa: of course this passage implies the existence and diffusion of drawings of private architecture in the society of the writer, probably either for the purpose of projects or for a dominius' knowledge about his own properties.

During the neosophistic period, descriptions of building are usually just the frame for the illustration of the *opera nobilia* which were exhibited there.

Thus in the *Amores* attributed to Lucian, there is a long description of the *naiskos* of the Cnidian Aphrodite (sections 13-17).

Pausanias in his *Periegesis* describes buildings in which masterpieces could be admired: in particular, the temples of Zeus and Hera and the *Philippeum* at Olympia and the temple of Apollo and the *lesche* of the Cnidians at Delphi are treated in great detail.

Philostratus the Elder also describes a *stoa* endowed with paintings.

With the sunset of the paganism, of course the *ekphrasis* focuses on different targets: for one landscapes rather than buildings are described. The best example of this genre is the 'Mosella' by Ausonius, in which he describes the landscapes which can be enjoyed along the Mosella river.

From the other side, the description and exaltation of the most admired Churches of the new cult becomes established. The *ekphrasis* enters a new flourishing period especially during the reigns of Anastasius I and of Justinian.

Paulus Silentiarius wrote an important description of the Church of St. Sophy at Constantinople, moreover Procopius from Caesarea in his *De aedificiis* describes more synthetically several constructions promoted or restored by Justinian both in Constantinople and in several other centres of the empire, finally three rhetors of the school of Gaza – John, Procopius of Gaza and Choricius – describe important monuments of their own city.[84]

---

[83] See R. Foertsch, *Archaeologischer Kommentar zu den Villenbriefen des Juengeren Plinius*, Mainz am Rhein (1993).
[84] See R. Talgam, 'The Ekphrasis eikonos of Procopius of Gaza, B. B. Ashkeloni (ed.), *Christian Gaza in late antiquity*, Leiden (2004) 209-234; I. Gualandri, 'Aspetti dell'ekphrasis in eta' tardoantica', *Testo e imagine nell'Alto Medioevo*, Spoleto (1994) 301-341; C. De Stefani, *Descriptio Sanctae Sophiae Descriptio Ambonis*

4. IMAGES ATTACHED TO ANCIENT DESCRIPTIONS OF ARCHITECTURES

In conclusion, there are not certain cases in which the *ekphrasis* of an architecture is accompanied by a drawing or by another visual instrument which helps the reader to imagine what is described.

That is logical because the same reason for the existence of the *ekphrasis* is the institution of a contest between the word and the image and the word is supposed to be greater than the image for expressive power as well as for its more widespread enjoyment by the public.

The only case of a reference to the drawing of a villa in a descriptive essay is in Pliny the Younger 5. 6. 13, however the mentioned drawing was not attached to the description of Pliny, but was the depiction of a villa whose function is not specified.

/ *Paulus Silentiarius*, Berlin (2011); V. Vavrinek, *Ekphrasis,* Prague (2011); J. Stenger, 'Chorikios und die Ekphrasis der Stephankirche von Gaza', *Janhrbuch Antike Christentum* 53 (2010) 81-103 and H. G. Thuemmel, 'Die Schilderung der Sergioskirche in Gaza und ihrer Dekoration bei Chorikios von Gaza', U. Lange (ed.), *Vom Orient bis an den Rhein*, Dettelback (1997) 49-64.

5. Miniature illustrations in Gromatic treatises

Now it is time to consider the *formae* which in the Roman world represented territories subjected to an official subdivision: in the Roman world, they were a sort of land registry and the gromatic writers often refer to them:[85] *centuriae*, funds which enjoyed a peculiar legal status, rivers, second ownerships and sometimes even territories outside official divisions were specified in these maps.

These *formae* were collected and copies of them were kept in the Imperial *tabularium*. The areas of the centuriations, the names of the landowners, the measures of the properties, perhaps even the type of crop, the not assigned lands, the demanial properties, the lands *excerpti* and given in concession, the lands which changed their functions, forests, meadows, rivers, mountains, sanctuaries, etc. were registered in these maps. Our gromatic sources who write of them do not specify which architectural works were represented.

However, maps of colonies do appear in manuscripts which contain gromatic essays. These maps are preserved in the *codex Arcerianus*, of the 6th c. in the *Codex Palatinus Latinus* 1564 of the 9th c. and in the *Codex Gudianus* 105 *Guelferbitanus* which is also of the 9th c. Several representations come from a lost archetype which collected gromatic treatises, which of course was earlier than the 6th c. and was illustrated.[86]

The first map represents the city of Suesa with its walls and towers, a temple and perhaps a palace in the middle of a centuriated territory and with the representation of *Mons Aricus*.

The second map represents Minturnum crossed by the *flumen Liris*, which flows into a water basin outside the city. To the right of the city the outline of the centuriation is drawn. Above it, the ridge of the *montes Vescini* are indicated, while at left there are a statue of a deity on a tall base, a hut with barrel vault and a tall building with a hexagonal plan whose function is uncertain. The walls of the city are also indicated with their towers and curtains

The third map represents Ispellum: as usual, it is defined with its circle of walls which on one side lay on a ridge of mountains forming a half circle. A river is represented as being sourced in this ridge of mountains and flowing toward the

---

[85] Ancient passages concerning these *formae* have been collected by F. Castagnoli, 'Le formae delle colonie romane e le miniature dei codici dei gromatici', *Atti della Reale Accademia d'Italia. Memorie della Classe di Scienze Morali e Storiche* 7. 4. 4 (1943) 83-118: as far as I know, this collection has not been substituted by a more recent one. About the Roman colonization, see S. Settis (ed.), *Misurare la terra*, Modena (2003).
[86] The considerations by Castagnoli (si veda nota 85) concerning this issue look to me conclusive.

side which is opposite to that the city: perhaps it is the Ose river. The centuriation is placed on the side opposite that of the city in reference to the ridge of mountains.

The fourth map is that of Terracina. This town is also represented through its city walls and it is crossed by two rivers, with the centuriated territory running along one side of the Via Appia. Both rivers flow into the sea, whose waves are indicated. Mountains occupy the background and the side opposed to that of the centuriation, arriving at the sea. The Pontine swamps are also indicated.

The fifth map is that of *Aventicum*: its squarish city walls with towers at the corners, curtains at the sides and a gate are indicated as well as two rivers, mountains and the centuriation.

The sixth map is that of *Augusta Bagiannorum*: the city walls are hexagonal, with towers at the corners and curtains at the sides, a ridge of mountains are developed on two sides of the city and the centuriation is indicated.

Finally a *Julia* colony is represented with rhomboid city walls, endowed with four gates, while the centuriation and the sea are not far away.

There are also two maps which are found only in the manuscripts *Palatinus* and *Gudianus*, of the 9th c. and which do not hark back to the archetype.

They are:

1. the map of Turin, and 2. That of a colony named *Augusta*: these have been recognized by Castagnoli as re-creations of hypothetic ancient Roman colonies, that can be attributed to the Carolingian classicism.

The conclusion of Castagnoli, that these maps derive from sources in the realm of ancient cartography, is based on conclusive reasons. These documents do not derive from architectural drawings.

6. References to architectural drawings in ancient literatures and inscriptions

We know from Vitruvius 1. 6. 12 that the technical word which defined the architectural drawing was *schema* and that it corresponded to the Latin *forma*.

This substantive in Greek has the main meaning of 'configuration, outline'[87] and is also a technical word of art criticism,[88] which designates the outline or silouette of a figure.

Moreover *schemata* are also named as the drawings of war machines and instruments in Apollodorus[89] and in Hero of Byzantium.[90] The *schema keimenon* is the drawing of the plan of a machine, while the *schema orthomenon* is the drawing of its elevation.[91]

Thus the semantic field covered by this word suggests that it had also had meanings in architectural drawings.

In Latin, this substantive also designates the illustration.[92]

A few words derived from *schema* are relevant to this research.

Schematographeo means 'I describe a figure': it is a verb of the technical terminology of mathematics as well as of mechanics, where it indicates the act of illustrating a machine with a figure.[93]

Similarly the *schematographia* is the drawing of the shape of a geometric or astronomic body, or of a map.[94]

Schematopoieo has a meaning not very different from that of *schematographeo* but it is a little more abstract.[95]

---

[87] See LSJ, *s. v.*
[88] See J. J. Pollitt, *The Ancient View of Greek Art*, New Haven (1974) 258-262 and M. L. Catoni, *Schemata*, Torino (2008) 19-317.
[89] See Apollodoro, *Poliorcetica* 137.
[90] See Hero, *Parangelmata Poliorcetica* 1 Wes. 199 and 27 Wes. 237: F. Sullivan, *Siegecraft*, Washington D. C. (2000) 154.
[91] See Hero, *Parangelmata Poliorcetica* 27 Wes. 237.
[92] See *Oxford Latin Dictionary*, *s. v.* About *formae* as 'projects', 'plans', see H. von Hesberg, 'Roemische Grundrissplaene aus Marmor', W. J. Brunner (a c. di), *Bauplanung und Bautheorie der Antike*, Berlin (1984) 120-133.
[93] See LSJ, *s. v.*
[94] See LSJ, *s. v.*
[95] See LSJ, *s. v.* This noun expresses the action of drawing a geometric figure (Procl., *In Eucl.* 111 F).

6. REFERENCES TO ARCHITECTURAL DRAWINGS IN ANCIENT LITERATURES AND INSCRIPTIONS

Vitruvius also provides words for specific architectural drawings.

Ichnographia (Vitruvius 1. 2. 2) is the plan of a building. The word is not found in Greek[96] nor in Latin[97] outside Vitruvius.

Vitruvius in the same passage specifies that *orthographia* means the drawing of the elevation of a building. Although this noun in Latin occurs frequently in the grammatical field, where it indicates the orthography, in the architectural field it is a *hapax*.[98] In Greek *orthographia* is used in grammar, again meaning the orthography,[99] but it is never evidenced in architecture. However the corresponding verb *orthographeo* means the act of drawing the elevation of a war machine in Apollodorus, *Poliorcetica* 193. 1.

Finally *scaenographia* according to Vitruvius 1. 2. 2 was the drawing which gives the sense of perspective to a building, expressing its third dimension and depth.

This noun is not evidenced in the surviving Latin written evidence outside Vitruvius,[100] while in Greek *schenographeo*, *schenographia* and *schenographikos* refer to the stage set, not to drawings of architecture seen from the point of view of perspective.[101]

We know from Vitruvius the the noun designating the architectural drawing in Latin was *forma* (the relevant Vitruvian passages have been quoted above in the section no. 2 of this essay).

This noun is used very often.[102] Among its many meanings, it means also geographic maps,[103] architectural drawings[104] maps of land registries and gromatic ones,[105] plans of military camps[106] and finally drawings of aqueducts.[107]

Cicero, *Ad Quintum fratrem* 2. 6. 3 mentions a *forma*, meaning the project of a *domus* under construction for his brother Quintus.

---

[96] See LSJ, *s. v.*
[97] See *Thesaurus linguae Latinae, s. v.*
[98] See *Thesaurus linguae Latinae, s. v.*
[99] See LSJ, *s. v.* and also *s. v. orthographos*.
[100] See *Oxford Latin Dictionary, s. v.*
[101] See LSJ, *s. vv.*
[102] See *Thesaurus linguae Latinae, s. v.*
[103] See *Thesaurus lunguae Latinae, s. v. Forma* iii A 1 b alpha.
[104] See *Thesaurus linguae Latinae, s. v. Forma* iii A 1 b beta: only passages of Vitruvius are cited. About *formae* as 'projects', 'plans', see von Hesberg (note 92) 120-133.
[105] See *Thesaurus linguae Latinae, s. v. Forma* iii A 1 b beta and gamma.
[106] Hyginus, *De munitionibus castrorum* 2. 15 and 23.
[107] Frontinus, *De aquaeductu Urbis Romae* 1. 17. 3-4 specifies that he ordered the making of drawings (*formae*) of Roman aqueducts for the need of his office.

Svetonius, *Divus Iulius* 31. 1 defines *forma* as a project for ephemeral constructions for the gladiatorial games of 49 B. C.

Still Svetonius, *Nero* 16. 1 remembers a *forma*, which in this case designates the project of the new type of buildings commissioned by Nero after the well know fire of Rome.

Tacitus, *Historiae* 4. 53 again uses *forma* with reference to the project of the temple of *Jupiter Optimus Maximus*.

Pliny the Younger, *Epistulae* 9. 39. 3-6 asks his friend Mustius for a *forma*, meaning a project, for a portico to be added to an old temple of Juno in his property.

Gellius 19. 10. 2-4 remembers several projects of baths for his friend Fronto: these projects were drawn on little pieces of parchment (*depictas in membranulis varias species balnearum*) and the patron selects the plan of the project of the building he prefers (*unam formam speciemque operis*), charging the architect with task.

A handheld *forma* is mentioned in an inscription of AD 2nd c. from *Africa Proconsularis* (*CIL* 8. 22788): probably even in this case it was the project of a building.

The project (*forma*) for an aqueduct of Antonine age is mentioned in an inscription from Lambesis (*CIL* 8. 2728).

Finally, there is the previously mentioned reference to the *forma picta* – a painted drawing – of a villa, which is frequently regarded by Pliny the Younger, *Epistulee* 5. 6. 13.

Vitruvius 1. 2. 2 and 1. 6. 12 refers to *schemata*, *ichnographia*, *orthographia* e *scaenographia* as widespread tools among architects of projects and attached 10 *formae* or drawings to his treatise (the passages *ad hoc* have been reported above).

Frontinus also testifies that preparing drawings of aqueducts was a duty of the office which was an important part of creating the structure (see note 107).

The *formae* of the military camps, which are known to Hyginus, are more similar to gromatic and colonial maps than to drawings of architecture.

6. REFERENCES TO ARCHITECTURAL DRAWINGS IN ANCIENT LITERATURES AND INSCRIPTIONS

Finally, plans and elevation of war machines were widespread at least from the age of Vitruvius, as the passages *ad hoc* of Apollodorus and Hero testify for the Roman imperial period.

In the epigraphic realm, the word *hypographe*, among its various meanings, appears to have that of 'drawing of a plan' in a couple of inscriptions.

In *ID* 500, lines 37 and 41, dated 297 B. C., from Delus, *hypographai* are mentioned in the Delian temple of Asclepios: probably they were drawings of plans on panels or *pinakes* dedicated in that building.

IvPri 207, dated to the late 3rd c. or early 2nd c. BC, from Priene, is the dedication by Hermogenes of the *hypographe* of a temple of which he had been architect in the famous temple of Athena at Priene.[108]

These inscriptions from Delus and Priene testify that drawings of plans of temples probably on panels or *pinakes* were a current tool in the Ionic world during the early and middle Hellenistic times and that, after the completion of the project, they were viewed as documents to be preserved and thus sometimes they were dedicated in temples.

Moreover the above cited passages of authours of the Roman period and the two above mentioned inscriptions from *Africa Proconsularis* testify to the widespread support for architectural projects in the Roman world from the late republican period until the Antonine age.

---

[108] See M. –C. Hellmann, *Recherches sur le vocabulaire de l'architecture grecque d'apres les inscriptions de Delos*, Atene (1992) 316-321. Other possible words which may indicate visual reproductions of architectural elements are evidenced in Attica in the epigraphic realm: *anagrapheus*, probably a metal leaf which reproduced mouldings made by architects for the making of these features by craftsmen (evidence in Merginesu (note 16) 12); *periteneia*, a surface on which the architect transfered his project and which was given to the subjected craftsmen (*ibidem*); finally the *metra*, which were metrological reliefs (*ibidem*). Marginesu supposes also that the word *gramma* means the drawing of the architectural project (*ibidem* 14).

7. Archaeological evidence of drawings of architecture

I am not aware of drawings of architecture dated before late classical times.

The examples I found are the following.

The representation with a drawing of a pediment is cut into a marble block from the lower rows of blocks of the cella of the temple of Athena at Priene (fig. 1): the drawing is attributed to Pytheos, the architect of the temple and is dated to the third quarter of the 4th c. BC.[109] Probably it was a drawing in the construction yard, prior to the building of one of the two pediments of the temple. Moreover preliminary drawings are cut on walls of the internal courtyard as well as on a wall of the pronaos of the temple of Apollo Philesius at Didyma and date to around 250 BC.[110] These cuts cover surfaces of around 2000 square feet[111] and in several cases have been recognized to be drawings of the following architectural elements:

    a. Of the vertical section of the entablature (fig. 2).[112]
    b. Of the vertical section of the frieze (fig. 3).[113]
    c. Of the vertical section of the Ionic column with the entasis (fig. 4).[114]

---

[109] See W. Koenigs, 'Der Athenatempel von Priene', *IstMitt* 33 (1983) 134-176, particularly 165-168 and 176, fig. 1; J. P. Heisel, *Antike Bauzeichnungen*, Darmstadt (1993) 158-159 and L. Haselberger, 'Architectural Likenesses', *JRA* 10 (1997) 77-94, particularly 81-82, fig. 6.
Incisions of vertical parallel lines linked with horizontal ones have been detected on a marble block of the cella of the temple of Athena at Priene (Heisel, cit. *supra* 167): perhaps they are too a drawing in the construction yard but no convincing explanation has been given which relates this drawing with a particular moment of the construction of the temple.
Preparatory incisions for the realization of triglyphs, rosettes, columns guttae, mutuli and geisa have been observed in the early archaic temple of Aphaia at Aegina (se E. –L. Schwandner, 'Zu Entwurf, Zeichnung und Maszsystem des aelteren Aphaiatempels von Aegina', J. –F. Bommelaer (ed.), *Le dessin d'architecture dans les societes antiques*, Strassburg (1985) 75-85). However these incisions are found exactly where these elements of the temple had to be built: thus they were part of the building process and should not be included among the project drawings of architecture. For this reason they have not been included among the examples discussed here.
[110] See L. Haselberger, 'Werkzeichnungen am Juengenren Didymaion', *IstMitt* 30 (1980) 191-215; Idem, Bericht ueber die Arbeit am Juengeneren Apollontempel von Didyma', *ibidem* 33 (1983) 90-123; Idem, 'Die Bauzeichnungen des Apollontempels auf Didyma', *Architectura* 13 (1983) 13-26; Idem, 'Die Werkzeichnungen des Naiskos im Apollontempel von Didyma', W. Hoepfner (ed.), *Bauplanung und Bautheorie der Antike*, Berlino (1984) 111-119; Idem, 'Die antiken Bauzeichnungen an dem Tempelwaenden des Apollon-Heiligtums in Didyma', *Nuernberger Blaetter zur Archaeologie* 5 (1988-1989) 31-33; Idem, 'Aspekte der Bauzeichnungen von Didyma', *RA* (1991) 99-113; Idem and H. Seybold, 'Seilkurve oder Ellipse?', *AA* (1991) 165-188; L. Haselberger, 'Antike Planzeichnungen am Apollontempel von Didyma', W. Hoepfner (ed.), *Fruehe Stadtkulturen*, Berlin (1997) 160-173; Idem, 'Architectural Likenesses', *JRA* 10 (1997) 77-94; Idem (note 58) 1-68; moreover Heisel (note 109) 167-183.
[111] See Haselberger, 'Architectural Likenesses' (note 110) 81.
[112] See Heisel (note 109) 169, no. G 3.
[113] See Heisel (note 109) 170, no. G 4.
[114] See Heisel (note 109) 171-173, no. G 5.

7. ARCHAEOLOGICAL EVIDENCE OF DRAWINGS OF ARCHITECTURES

    d. Of the vertical section of the shaft of a column with its entasis (fig. 5).[115]
    e. Of the horizontal section of half of a column (fig. 6).[116]
    f. Of the horizontal section of a quarter of a column (fig. 7).[117]
    g. Of a rosette placed with a system of circles (fig. 8).[118]
    h. Finally of the horizontal and vertical lines composing a panel of a ceiling (fig. 9).[119]

The interpretation of these cuts as drawings in the construction yard is convincing. Thus these drawings were an intermediate moment between the comprehensive preliminary project, of which these incisions were partial copies, and the actual construction of the various architectural elements. This observation leads to the conclusion that these drawings are visual evidence of the preliminary study and planning of the temple.

Architectural drawings are also in evidence in Ptolemaic Egypt.

It is necessary to specify that in Egypt the tradition of architectural drawings was very ancient and harked back to the 3rd millennium BC:[120] tombs, gardens, storerooms, temples, sanctuaries, pyramids, fields, quarries, capitals, columns, vaults, windows and doors were represented, usually in plan but sometimes also in elevation, on stone, sandstone, papyri, rock, plaster, limestone, slate, clay and painted walls.

Thus the architectural drawings of Ptolemaic Egypt are rooted on a habit which had a long tradition.

During the reign of Ptolemaeus IX (116-81 B. C.), in the Iseum of Philae the horizontal section of a lower shaft (fig. 10)[121] and the vertical one of a column (fig. 11)[122] are incised on stone. Still during the late Ptolemaic period, the upper end of two flutes of column (fig. 12)[123] were incised on stone in the temple of Horus at Edfu.

These examples of the Ptolemaic period are also drawings in construction yards.

---

[115] See Heisel (note 109) 173-174, no. G 6.
[116] See Heisel (note 109) 174-175, no. G 7.
[117] See Heisel (note 109) 175, no. G 8.
[118] See Haselberger, 'Aspekte, etc.' (note 110) 103, fig. 4.
[119] See Haselberger, 'Aspekte, etc.' (note 110) 106, fig. 7.
[120] See Heisel (note 109) 76-153: he collects 24 examples of architectural drawings for Egypt before the Ptolemaeans.
[121] See Heisel (note 109) 139, no. Ae 25. We should remember also the drawing on papyrus *PLille* 1 of 259-258 B. C. which represents a plan for terracing works. Although it has a topographical rather than architectural value, it is necessary not to forget it even in this essay. See Settis (note 1) 581-606, particularly 588.
[122] See Heisel (note 109) 140-141, no. Ae 26.
[123] See Heisel (note 109) 141-142, no. Ae 27.

In the Seleucid middle east, the Mesopotamic tradition of architectural drawings cut on clay tablets continues:[124] in the pre-Seleucid age, houses, temples, cities, sanctuaries, storerooms, zikkurat, palaces, fields and ladders were represented, usually on clay *pinakes*, less often on diorite supports or with reliefs on stone.

In Hellenistic Susa, two clay tablets bearing architectural drawings have been found: they represented two plans of a possible *forica* (fig. 13)[125] and of a probable temple (fig. 14):[126] they may have been legal documents or land registers.

During the Augustan period, the tradition of architectural drawings continues in Egypt.

The drawing of a capital (fig. 15) was found in the temple of Mandulis at Bab – al – Kalabsha, in Nubia, which dates 30 B. C.[127] In the same architectural context, a drawing of an Egyptian column, with its typical fan-shape capital, is found (fig. 16).[128]

In the same period, two drawings from the stone quarry of Gebel Abu Foda are dated: one represents a lotus capital (fig. 17),[129] the other a Hator capital included in an orthogonal grid (fig. 18).[130]

In the same period, at Meidun, the drawing of the diagonal line of a pyramid was incised: (fig. 19)[131] the inclination of this line coincides with that of the pyramid no. 2 of Meroe.

These examples appear also to be drawings in construction yards.

Still in Egypt, the plan of a house (fig. 20) is drawn on a papyrus from Oxyrhynchus (*POxy* 24. 2406) of Hadrianic – Antonine age, which also provides the size of the rooms:[132] it was probably a property document which may have been required for a legal contract.

The upper sections of two unfluted columns with their Corinthian capitals, supporting an architrave with upper border and a frieze decorated with shoots of acanthus, are represented on another papyrus from Oxyrhynchus (*POxy* 71.

---

[124] See Heisel (note 109) 7-75: 41 examples of pre-Hellenistic architectural drawings from the middle east are collected.
[125] See Heisel (note 109) 50-51, no. M 42.
[126] See Heisel (note 109) 51, no. M 43.
[127] See Heisel (note 109) 142-143, no. Ae 28.
[128] See Heisel (note 109) 143, no. Ae 29.
[129] See Heisel (nota 109) 143-144, no. Ae 30.
[130] See Heisel (note 109) 144, no. Ae 31.
[131] See Heisel (nota 109) 145-146, no. Ae 32.
[132] See Haselberger, 'Architectural Likenesses' (note 110) 88, fig. 15 and Settis (note 121) 588.

7. ARCHAEOLOGICAL EVIDENCE OF DRAWINGS OF ARCHITECTURES

4842) (fig. 21), dated around AD 140. J. J. Coulton, who published this important document,[133] noticed that both architrave and frieze are too high when compared to their capitals, and that these shoots of acanthus in the frieze of this entablature are unparalleled in real architecture and concluded that probably the creator had been inspired by an architectural order applied to an object.

Nevertheless, this papyrus reveals the importance of the practice of drawing architectural elements on papyri in the visual culture of Egypt in the middle imperial period, although the specific function of this drawing cannot be specified.

Architectural drawings are not unknown in Roman imperial Syria.

At the Ionic temple of Bziza, in northern Lebanon, in Hadrianic – Antonine times, two drawings are incised: one represents the pediment of a temple (fig. 22)[134] while the other shows the vertical section of the entablature (fig. 23).[135]

At Baalbek, on the W side of the podium of the temple of Jupiter, a pediment is incised (fig. 24): it corresponds to the S section of the back pediment of the temple. These cuts probably are of Julio-Claudian age, when the temple of Jupiter was built.[136]

Another drawing is incised on the S side of the retaining wall of the sanctuary of Jupiter, in front of the N side of the temple of Bacchus: it represents the vertical section of an entablature supporting a concave roof (fig. 25), most probably the entablature and roof of a fountain near the temple of Bacchus.[137] The drawing is Antonine as this temple.

Moreover a triangular shape and an arc of a circle are incised on the N anta of the flying steps in front of the temple of Bacchus (fig. 25).

Two other drawings have been found on the pavement of the large courtyard, between the small altar and the flying steps in front of the temple of Jupiter: they are two arcs of circles (fig. 26), probably share the date of the pavement and thus are Trajanic.

Finally, on an exedra in the N part of the sanctuary, other two architectural drawings have been recognized: the first represents the NW section of the plan of the hexagonal courtyard (fig. 27), the other shows a vault (fig. 28) which

---

[133] See J. J. Coulton, in H. Whitehouse, 'Drawing a fine line in Oxyrhynchus', A. K. Bowman, *Oxyrhynchus*, London (2007) 296-306, particularly 304-306.
[134] See Heisel (note 109) 211-212, no. R 14, and Haselberger, 'Architectural likenesses', etc. (note 110) 88-89.
[135] See Heisel (note 109) 211-213, no. R 15.
[136] See Heisel (note 109) 213, no. R 16.
[137] See Heisel (note 109) 213-214, no. R 17.

corresponds to the barrel vault above the central part of the room where these incisions are located. They date to the period of completion of the hexagonal courtyard, which is attributed to Philip the Arab.[138]

Of course these examples of Roman imperial age from the Syrian region are drawings in construction yards and reveal the noteworthy presence of this practice from around AD 50 to around AD 250, throughout two centuries.

In Asia Minor, the practice of making drawings in contruction yards, after the late classical and Hellenistic examples of Priene and Didyma, is also known for the Roman imperial period, thanks to two incised drawings from Pergamon: both are pertinent to the Ionic temple on the terrace of the theatre in its AD 2nd c. phase: in one of these drawings the vertical section of a column is represented (fig. 29)[139] while the other represents the left corner of the entablature of the façade in its previous Hellenistic phase (fig. 30): this front had been destroyed by a fire and was about to be restored with a new front.[140] In both cases, they are probably remainders of elements of the previous façade which had to be restored during the rebuilding of the frontal section of the temple.

During the Roman imperial period, architectural drawings are also much in evidence in the central Mediterranean region.

At Rome, in the area in front of the Mausoleum of Augustus, drawings of an abacus of a Corinthian pillar capital (fig. 31), of a pediment and of the right corner of a frontal entablature (fig. 32) have been noticed and the latter has been recognized to represent the corresponding element of the pronaos of the Pantheon.[141]

These incisions look homogeneous and since one of these three drawings has been identified with a part of the Hadrianic Pantheon, it is likely that these are drawings for builders of the Hadrianic period and that the third drawing was preparatory to the building of the facade of the pronaos of the Pantheon.

In the *I regio* of Italy, *Latium et Campania*, three other drawings in a construction yard have been recognized in the large amphitheater of Capua and they appear to be pertinent to its Hadrianic-Antonine phase: they represent an arch (fig. 33), which can be identified as an arch of the lower external order of the amphitheater,[142] as

---

[138] About the architectural drawings in the sanctuaries of Jupiter and Bacchus at Baalbek, see D. Lohmann, 'Drafting and Designing', K. E. Kurrer (ed.), *Proceedings of the Third International Congress on Construction History*, Cottbus (2009) 959-966.
[139] See Heisel (note 109) 208-209, no. R 10.
[140] See Haselberger, 'Architectural Likenesses' (note 110) 86-87.
[141] See L. Haselberger, 'Ein Giebelriss der Vorhalle des Pantheon', *RM* 101 (1994) 279-308 and Idem, 'Architectural Likenesses' (note 110) 88-89.
[142] See Heisel (note 109) 210, no. R 11.

7. Archaeological evidence of drawings of architectures

well as various geometric patterns (figs. 34-35).[143] These drawings probably had been made in view of the reconstruction of a section of the external arcade in the Hadrianic-Antonine times as well as of the accomplishment of its decorative display.

In the *X regio* of Italy, *Venetia et Histria*, at Pola, a drawing representing the sequence of an external inferior arcade of the amphitheater (fig. 36) is incised on the base of the third pillar W of the main entrance to the monument.[144] This drawing may have been done in view of the restoration of part of the external inferior order of the amphitheater which occurred during the reign of Vespasian.

A marble slab with the incised drawing of a volute (fig. 37) was found at Thysdrus in *Africa Proconsularis* and dates to AD 2nd c. (it is kept in the museum attached to the Seminar of Classical Archaeology of the University of Bern):[145] it probably was a mobile *pinax*, used as an instruction to craftsmen about how to make a volute.

The Roman world, beside drawings in construction yards, which usually are incisions of architectural elements on stone supports, also used drawings of plans of building complexes.

Drawn representations of cities, of elements of the urban grid, as well as of building complexes had been not unknown to the Mesopotanian world[146] or to Egypt.[147]

At Rome, the land register of the city was obtained through drawings incised on bronze slabs of which marble copies survive: these derivative drawings date from the Julio-Claudian age to the Severan one (*formae Urbis Romae*): these marble copies of the Roman land register were made by an office of the *Praefectura urbana* which was in charge of the representation of the territory for the purpose of taxation.

Marble panels which show specific cadastral units have also been found, usually they also give the names of their owners, and gives figures of the sizes of the rooms of properties, in order to determine their taxable wealth and their

---

[143] See Heisel (note 109) 210-211, nos. R 12 e R 13.
[144] See Haselberger, 'Architectural Likenesses' (note 110) 82-83.
[145] See T. Loertscher, 'Voluta constructa', *Antike Kunst* 32 (1989) 82-103; Heisel (note 109) 214-216, no. R 18 and Haselberger, 'Architectural Likenesses' (note 110) 91-92.
[146] See Heisel (note 109) 9-75: whilst drawings of architectural complexes hark back to the Akkadic culture (Heisel 10-17, nos. M 1-10 from Tello), the first surviving representation of a city dates around 1500 BC, and comes from Nippur (Heisel 37, no. M 30).
[147] See Heisel (notae109) 79-138: whilst drawings of buildings are known from the period of the 3rd dynasty onwards (Heisel 80, no. Ae 1), on the contrary drawing representations of larger areas are known from the 18th dynasty onwards (Heisel 88, no. Ae 5).

contributions: these *pinakes* were copies of the cartography of the land registry of Rome (figs. 38-48).[148] These marble pictures were placed on walls of the represented properties and may have worked both as property documents as well as expressions of the prosperity of their owners. The surviving examples provide schematic plans made with incised drawings of the related buildings as well as of the surrounding territories.[149]

These *formae* were also made for other cities beside Rome, as it is argued by the above considered illustrations of gromatic treatises as well as by the *forma* of the city of *Aguntum*, rom the Severan period (fig. 49),[150] which also provides incised drawings of plans of the most important buildings in the city.

A lithic *forma* from the *hortus* of the Church of St. Mary on Mt. Aventinus represents with an incised drawing the route of an aqueduct inside the city (fig. 50) and specifies the names of owners of the land through which the aqueduct was going, as well as the timetable when each landowner could draw water:[151] this document confirms the existence of *formae* of aqueducts which is known thanks to Frontin.

There are also drawn representations of architectural complexes on mosaic pavements: the most important example is a late AD 2nd c. mosaic from Marsala street in Rome, now kept in the Antiquarium of Mt. Caelius (fig. 51), which represents the *balneum* where it was found:[152] even in this case the rooms of the baths are provided with numbers, given in feet, of their length and width. In this case, it is probable that the representaton of these baths of the land register was transferred to a mosaic instead of being reproduced in a panel destined to be placed on a wall of the building complex.

Another drawing plan on a mosaic from Ostia (fig. 52) represents more synthetically the funerary yard which was adjacent to this pavement:[153] the owner probably wanted to give emphasis to his own tombs with their monumental dignity.

Finally a circus, which has been identified with the Circus Maximus of Rome, is represented with a drawing on an AD 5th c. mosaic in the House of Mosaics of

---

[148] See R. Meneghini and R. Santangeli Valenzani (ed,), *Formae Urbis Romae*, Roma (2006) particularly 30-39 e 166-171; E. D'Ambrosio *et alii*, 'Nuovi frammenti di piante marmoree', *BullComm* 112 (2011) 67-76 and R. Tucci, 'The Marble Plan on the Via Anicia', *BSR* 81 (2013) 90-127.
[149] A complete catalogue of these marble fragments is found in the bibliography cited in note 148.
[150] See Heisel (note 109) 197-199, no. R 7.
[151] See Heisel (note 109) 185-186, no. R 1.
[152] See A. Bouet, 'La mosaique de la via Marsala a Rome (Regio V)', *MEFRA* 110 (1998) 849-892 and Meneghini and Santangeli Valenzani (note 148) 36.
[153] See Heisel (note 109) 192-193, no. R 5.

7. ARCHAEOLOGICAL EVIDENCE OF DRAWINGS OF ARCHITECTURES

Luni (fig. 53):[154] perhaps it reveals the interest of the landowner for performances in circuses or the celebration of one of the most important monuments of Rome in an age – that of Rutilius Namantianus – when the veneration of the most renowned architecture of the *Urbs* was very deeply felt.

Finally few drawings of architectural subjects with an artistic purpose are also evidenced.

At Pompeii, in the Julio-Claudian period, in the Citarista's House (= I. 4. 5. 25), triclinium no. 19 was decorated – in the platform of the E section of the S wall – with a drawing of a garden with fences, pergolas and aviaries made of lathing (fig. 54).[155] This drawing was not the preliminary work for a painting but appeared in this way when the decoration of this room was completed.

On the contrary, in the House of Ceres, also at Pompeii (= I. 9. 13), in the central section of the S wall of the cubiculus k, there is the drawing in red ochre of a Corinthian capital: probably it was a preliminary test in view of the painting of this pattern (fig. 55). The drawing of this capital is dated in the phase of 2nd style of the decoration of this domus, thus in the advanced 1st c. BC.[156]

---

[154] See P. Ciancio Rossetto, 'Il nuovo frammento della *Forma* severiana rinvenuto al Circo Massimo', Meneghini and Santangeli Valenzani (note 148) 127-141, particularly 135-137.
[155] See M. de Vos, 'I 4, 5. 25 Casa del Citarista', G. Pugliese Carratelli (ed.), *Pompei pitture e mosaici* 1, Rome (1990) 117-177, particularly 148, no. 53.
[156] See M. de Vos, 'I 9, 13 Casa di Cerere', Pugliese Carratelli (note 155) 2. 172-229, particularly 222-223, no. 77.

8. Conclusions

I. Chronology of the evidence

The documents which testify to the *genus* of drawings which are known from the 4th century BC onwards include: the project submitted by Dinocrates to Alexander concerning the transformation of Mt. Athos into a city, narrated by Vitruvius, as well as the drawing of a pediment from the Athenaion of Priene are in fact the first surviving examples of that type of drawing. This circumstance does not mean that there were not drawings of architecture prior to 350-330 BC: on the contrary it is probable that at least the architecture of the archaic and classical period, which imply a previous careful theoretical study, and particularly those which had been objects of treatises written by their architects, were based on project drawings. However these drawings have not survived and the same treatises of architects who planned these important buildings are lost.

Although we have only literary and epigraphical records of project drawings, it is probable that in the classical period they were drawn on papyri, since this conclusion is suggested by the comparison with plans of whole buildings drawn on papyri in the Egyptian world.[157] Another possibility is that the Mesopotamic practice of drawings of buildings incised on clay *pinakes* had been introduced into the Greek world. The use of marble *pinakes* as material supports of incised drawings of architecture, which is well evidenced in the Roman world, may perhaps be suggested as well for the Greek world.

Drawings in construction yards, which are known from the example of Priene onwards, may have been copied from those project drawings.

They may have worked as reminders of the single elements of the building which had to be achieved and probably were incised either by craftsmen or by the architect who may have explained to his workers what to do with these visual representations.

In the Hellenistic period in the Aegean world, projects of whole buildings are recorded by inscriptions, precisely by the above mentioned dedications of documents of that genre in the Asklepieion of Delos and in the Athenaion of Priene: in the last case the dedicant was Hermogenes.

---

[157] See Heisel (note 109) examples nos. Ae 3, Ae 12, Ae 15, Ae 19 and Ae 20.

8. Conclusions

The fact that these drawings were dedicated in sanctuaries implies that they were regarded as important, documents to be preserved even after the construction of the actual buildings, as materials to be kept in archives.

Drawings in contruction yards are well known thanks to the rich evidence from the Didymaion.

They are known also in the Ptolemaic world, in continuity with the rooting of this practice in Egypt that was already happening in the pre-Alexandrian period. In the 1st century BC, there is evidence even in Nubia.

In the Seleucid world, the pre-Hellenistic tradition of representing buildings on clay tablets continues: these *pinakes* probably had legal functions (documents of property?) or were made for the land registry.

At Rome, project drawings of buildings are recorded in the literary tradition and by a few inscriptions: the known cases range chronologically from the age of Caesar to the Antonine one.

In one case (Gellius 19. 10. 2-4) the material support of these projects is specified: the parchment.

During the Roman imperial period, the production of the *formae urbis* comes to a head: these were representations of the territory of the city for taxation. The official drafting of these documents was in bronze but these bronze *pinakes* are not preserved. However we have marble copies of them.

Marble *pinakes* reproduced specific cadastral units and could be used as property documents or be 'shown' as evidence of the economic prosperity of their owners.

Drawings of architectural elements in construction yards are well evidenced as well in the Roman world, particularly in the Hadrianic-Antonine age: at Rome, Capua, Pola, Pergamum, Bziza, Baalbek, etc.

The marble panel bearing an incised volute from Thysdrus is also noteworthy, because it is the only surviving document of the use of incising drawings of architectural details on mobile supports which could be taken to wherever they were found useful.

Drawings of architecture on papyri are evidenced in Egypt in the middle imperial period thanks to two papyri from Oxyrhynchus: on one of them the plan of a house is shown, and probably is a property document, while on the other a portico is represented: the latter example may have been an artistic drawing without a specific function.

From the late AD 2nd century drawings of buildings are represented on mosaics: at Rome and Ostia the same complexes adorned with these mosaics are represented that way, probably because their owners wanted to give emphasis to the importance and beauty of their properties and perhaps also because they wanted to celebrate their wealth.

In the case of the mosaic with the drawing of a circus at Luni in AD 5th century, it is possible to hypothesize the interest of the patron for the represented circus. However it is also possible that this mosaic shows the admiration for one of the most renowned monuments in Rome: the Circus Maximus.

The artistic drawing, *i. e.* the representation of architectural details with drawings without specific functions and not as preliminary phase for the accomplishment of other works of art such as paintings is rare but is found at Pompeii as well as on a papyrus from Oxyrhynchus.

Finally, the above mentioned mosaic from Luni is at the beginning of the tradition to reproduce with drawings the most renowned monuments of Rome.

II. What drawings of architecture looked like

Project drawings are known only from the written tradition and thus it is possible only to forward hypotheses about what they looked like.

If we accept the probability that several drawings from construction yards derived from those projects, we should argue that the architectural elements represented were reproduced to scale. Exact place, dimensions and modular relations were specified with horizontal, vertical and curved lines sketched with the compass.

Drawings in construction yards show especially how elements of the elevation of a building were made.

Concerning the plans of buildings, we should look on representations of blocks from cities, especially Rome, as well as on the above mentioned plan of a house from Oxyrhynchus. In these documents, the plans of buildings represented are reproduced to scale and the most important dimensions of the rooms are provided. We can guess that the same use also characterized project drawings.

8. Conclusions

We do not know what drawings of fronts of buildings that also gave the sense of their depth looked like. These documents are known thanks to Vitruvius but are visually unknown.

Equally, drawings of architecture illustrating books, mentioned several times by Vitruvius, are not known.

However it has to be noticed that Vitruvius refers to two illustrations – about how to make the entasis of a column and how to make a volute – which are known also thanks to a drawing from the construction yard of the Didymaion and to a marble panel from Thysdrus.

Thus it is possible that the two book illustrations cited were not very different from known drawings of the same subjects.

Of course it is equally probable that drawings attached to architectural treatises were 'sources' of imitation for drawings from construction yards, although it is likely that book illustrations were more sophisticated than construction drawings.

We should also consider the drawings representing land areas, usually of cities.

It is probable that they differed from project plans especially because, even when they represented a single block, the names of their landowners were registered.

Moreover the frequent representation of plans of whole areas of cities or even of whole cities is another salient feature of these *formae*.

Only a few examples are known of drawings of architecture made for artistic purposes. It seems that artistic drawings differed from other *genera* of architectural drawings by their absence of practical functions and because they appear to have been rather free from the modular and proportional concerns which characterized both drawings in construction yards and representations of city's land districts.

III. Functions of architectural drawings

The following functions can be attributed to drawings of architecture in the Greek-Roman world on the basis of the collected evidence:

1. Project of a building.
2. Reminder in a construction yard.
3. Representation of land areas of a city for reasons of taxation and/or of land registry.
4. Document of property (see examples from Oxyrhynchus, Perugia, Urbino, etc.).

5. Artistic representation (see the Corinthian porch on a paryrus from Oxyrhynchus and the garden drawn at Pompeii).
6. Finally, and only in late antiquity, a drawn copy of a renowned monument, if the circus on a mosaic from Luni is to be interpreted that way.

IV. Critical deductions

The project drawings of buildings confirm that ancient architecture, or at least its most prestigious quarter, was based on a theoretical background and on careful preliminary studies.

Thus they clarify that the function of the architect, at least from the late classical period onwards, was first of all that of planner and designer and only afterwards that of master builder.[158]

Even drawings in construction yards are important not only for their contribution to the 'archaeological' knowledge of the monument on which they have been incised, but also because they often bear modular indications and thus reveal that even craftsmen charged with making the buildings had fully assimilated the modular culture of the architects in charge as well as the idea that a building must conform to a previously conceived 'model'.

The artistic drawing of architecture is also known, although in few *exempla*: there were 'free' drawings of buildings and 'ideal' environments which do not coincide with known monuments and thus were plausible but not necessarily real creations; moreover the copy of a renowned monument also existed.

Thus it is necessary to conclude that these two genres of drawings, which are so well known from the late medieval culture onwards, already existed in the ancient world, at least in the Roman imperial times.

Finally drawings made in order to represent private properties or land areas of cities, for legal purposes or for land registries or for taxation, usually take the shape of plans, often endowed with dimensions of rooms, and thus provide important evidence for the knowledge of legal changes of property of the real estate as well as of the state administration of the taxation of the Roman imperial age. This branch of the state had access to a very detailed knowledge – nearly *ad unguem* – of the real estate of a city and thus had enough data in order to decide with precision and fairness the taxes which landowners had to pay.

---

[158] About the debate concerning the professional figure of the architect, see H. Eiteljorg, 'The Architect in Classical Architecture', X. M. A Vila *et alii* (eds.), *Archaeotecture*, Oxford (2003) 107-112 and C. Anderson, 'Architect and Patron', R. B. Ulrich (ed.), *A Companion to Roman Architecture*, New York (2014) 127-139 with previous bibliography.

9. Catalogue of drawings of architecture in the Greek and Roman world

Keys to the interpretation of the catalogue's entries:

1. Title.

2. Description.

3. Collocation.

4. Date.

5. Material support.

6. Technique.

7. Dimensions.

8. Bibliography.

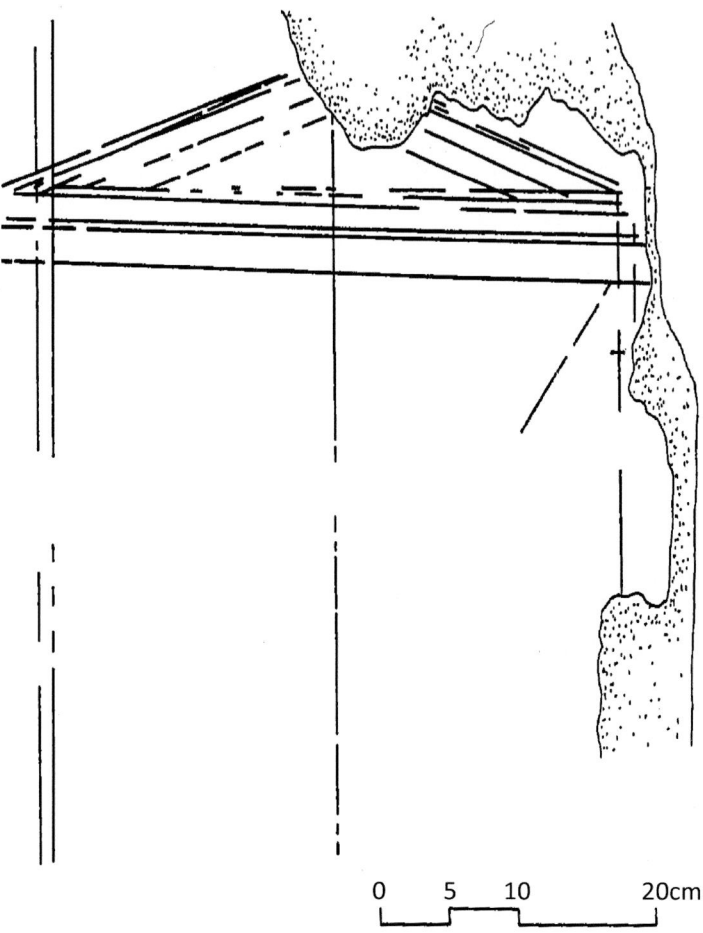

1.

1. Pediment
2. The drawing represents a pediment with a rather clear outline of its triangular shape. The simae – both horizontal and oblique – are well marked with line segments. Below the horizontal sima, another horizontal line segment probably marks the geison. A vertical segment, drawn from the top of the pediment, divides the gable in due parts. The corners of the pediment are also marked by double vertical segments.
3. Priene, temple of Athena, from the lower section of the cella.
4. Third quarter of the 4th century BC.
5. Stone wall.
6. Incision.
7. 34 x 38 cm.
8. Koenigs, Heisel and Haselberger (nota 109).

9. CATALOGUE OF DRAWINGS OF ARCHITECTURES IN THE GREEK AND ROMAN WORLD

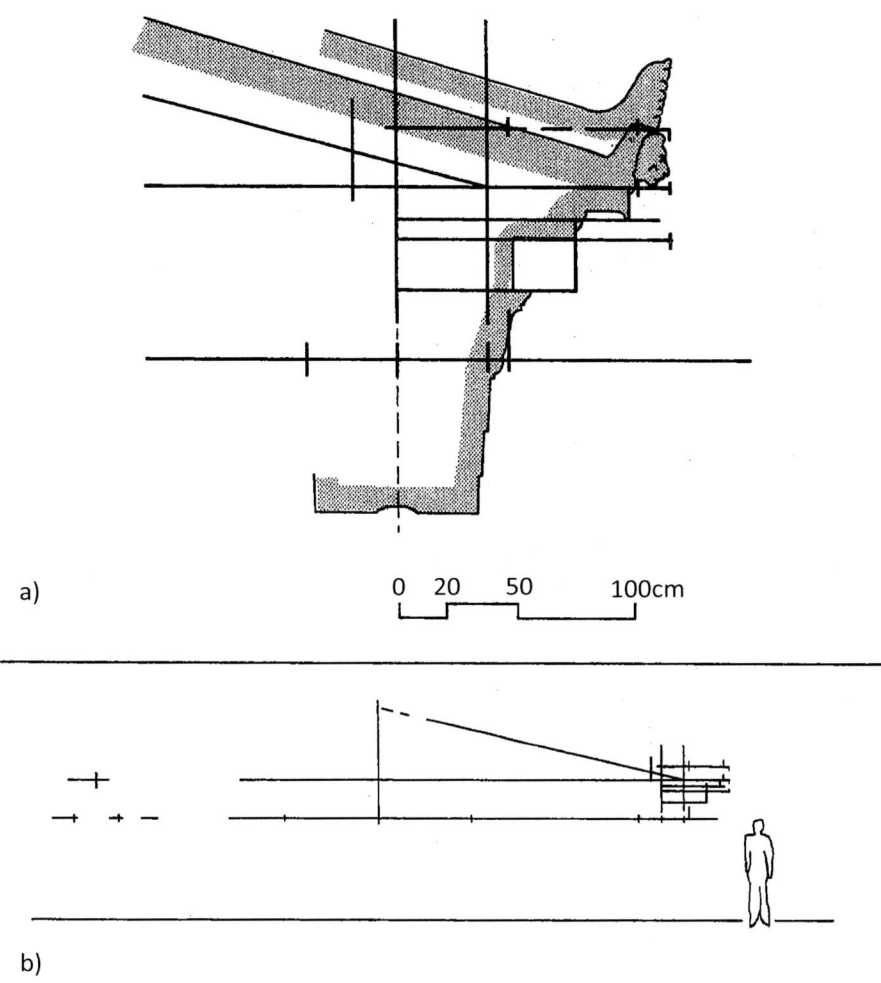

a)

b)

2.

1. Vertical section of entablature.
2. The drawing represents a pediment, whose oblique diretrix from the viewer's right is marked with a line segment. Horizontal parallel segments mark the height of the oblique sima, of the horizontal sima and of the lower elements of the entablature. The vertical directrix divides the gable in two parts from the top of the pediment. Two vertical segments relate the elements of the entablature to the inclination of the pediment.
3. Didyma, temple of Apollo, baseboard of the W wall of the adyton.
4. Around 250 BC
5. Stone wall
6. Incision.
7. 1200 x 200 cm.
8. Heisel (note 112).

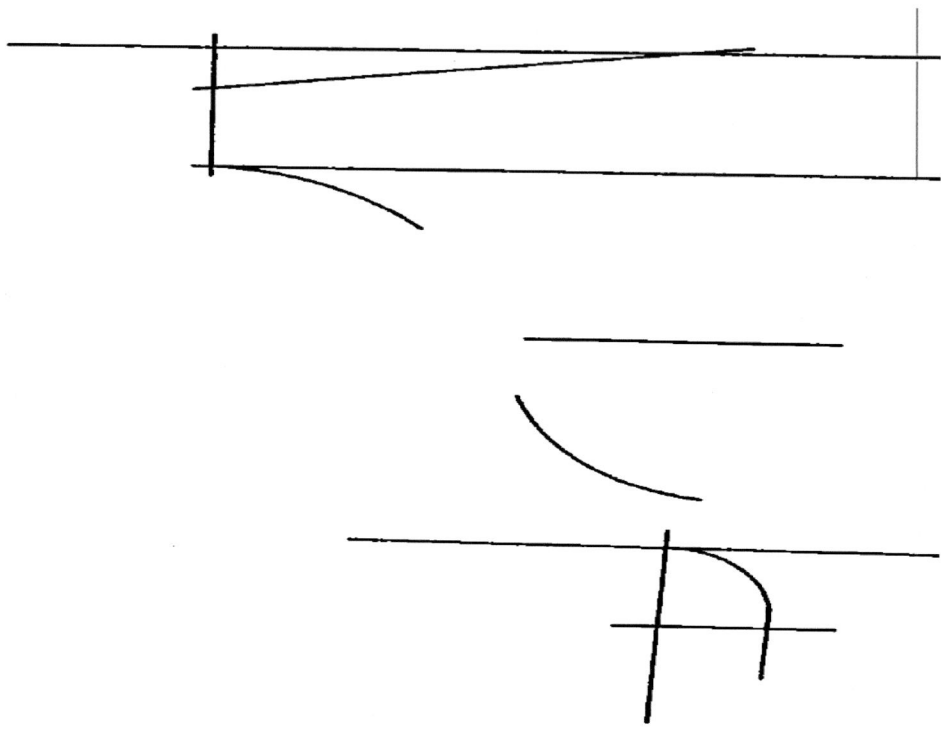

3.

1. 1. Vertical section of frieze.
2. 2. Corner profile of the entablature below the horizontal sima marked with horizontal parallel segments. A vertical segment marks the angular ending of the cornice and curved lines mark the profiles of the lower mouldings.
3. 3. Didyma, temple of Apollo, N wall of the sekos.
4. 4. Around 250 BC
5. 5. Stone wall.
6. 6. Incision.
7. 7. Dimensions not given.
8. 8. Heisel (note 113).

9. CATALOGUE OF DRAWINGS OF ARCHITECTURES IN THE GREEK AND ROMAN WORLD 57

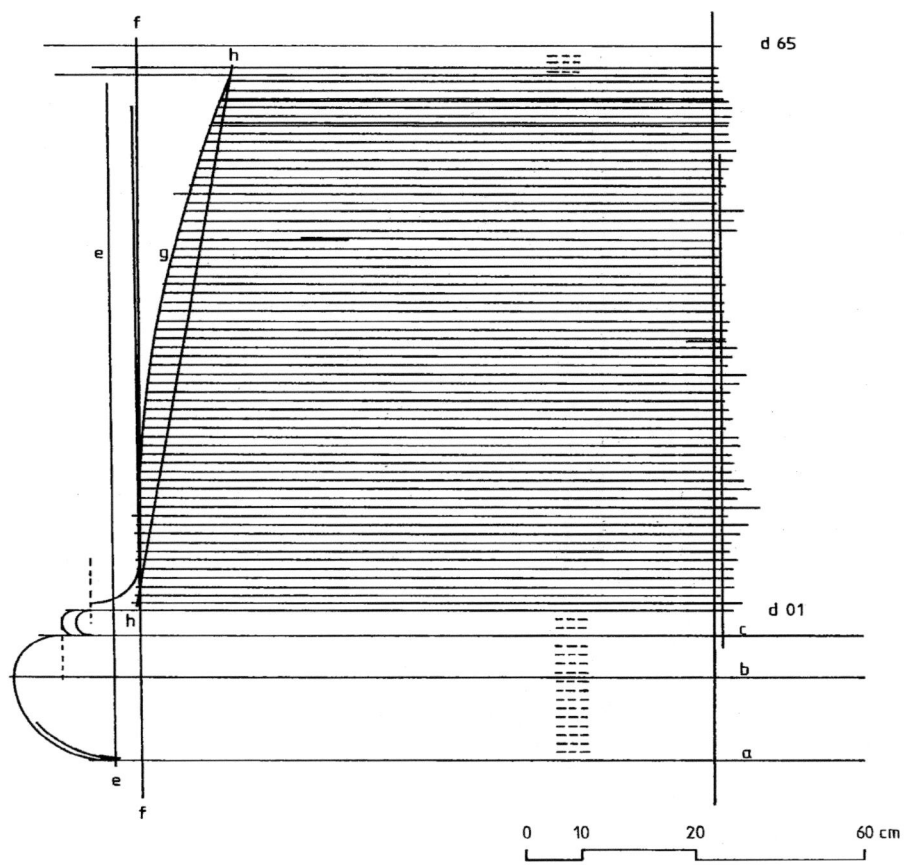

4.

1. Vertical section of Ionic column with entasis.
2. The drawing represents the curved profile of the torus. Its horizontal inferior border and the horizontal directrix at the point of greater projection of the torus are also indicated. Another slightly oblique segment perhaps represents the inclination of the horizontal lines of the temple. Above the torus, the vertical axis of the column, the vertical line corresponding to the ending of the lower shaft, the oblique directrix of the tapering and the curved one of the entasis are also indicated. The column is divided among many horizontal segments: probably they made easier the calculation of the entasis.
3. Didyma, temple of Apollo, baseboard, near the E corner of the N wall of the adyton.
4. Around 250 BC.
5. Stone wall.
6. Incision.
7. 160 x 130 cm.
8. Heisel (note 114).

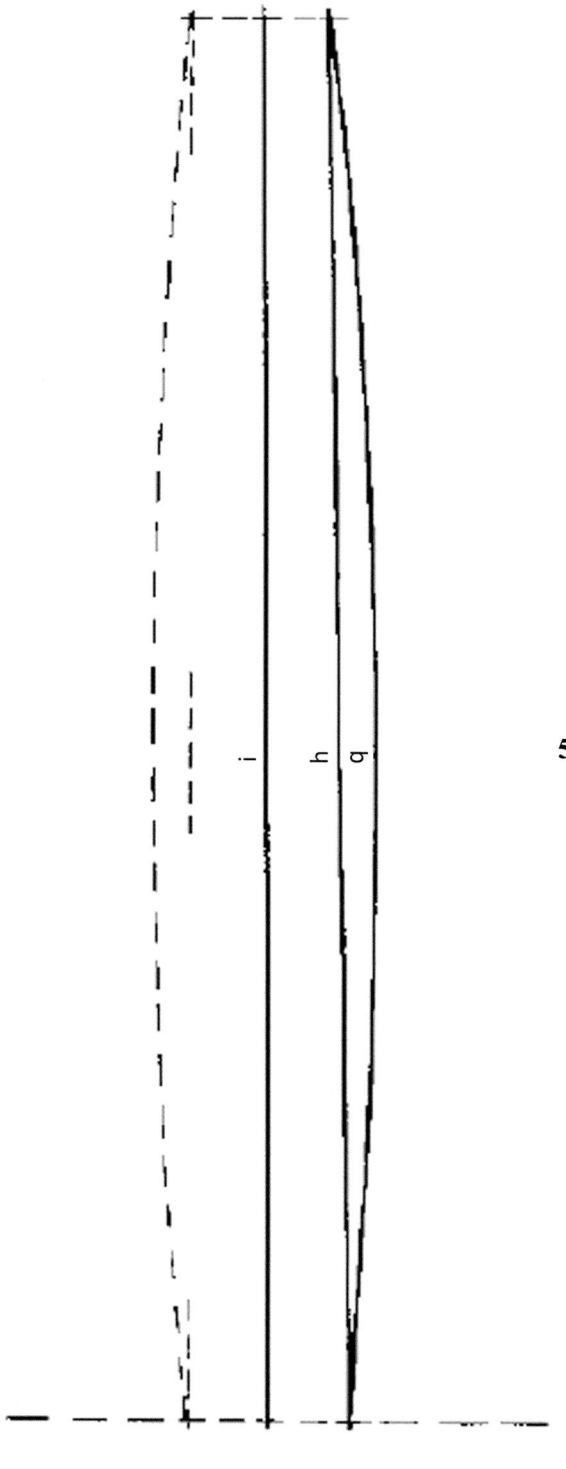

5.
1. Vertical section of shaft of column with entasis.
2. The drawing represents the vertical section of the shaft: dotted lines indicate the horizontal directrixes of the lower shaft and of the upper shaft and segments indicate the axis of the column, an external vertical directrix and the related curvatures.
3. Didyma, temple of Apollo, baseboard of the N wall of the adyton.
4. Around 250 BC
5. Stone wall
6. Incision.
7. 1820 x 101, 4 cm.
8. Heisel (note 115).

9. Catalogue of drawings of architectures in the Greek and Roman world

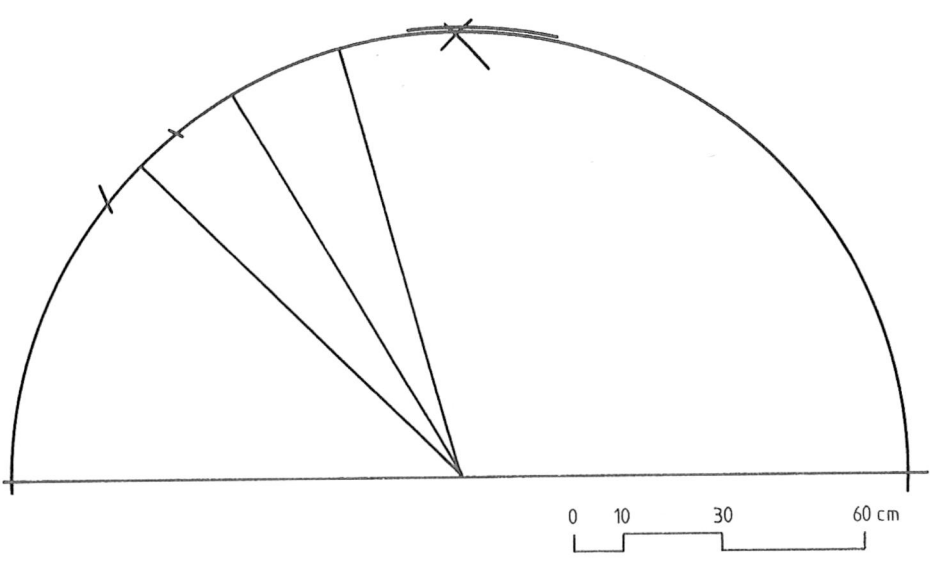

6.

1. Horizontal section of semicolumn.
2. The diameter of a semicolumn, the semicircumference, the chord, two arcs of circle are drawn and the center of the semicircumference is signed.
3. Didyma, temple of Apollo, baseboard of the N wall of the adyton.
4. Around 250 BC.
5. Stone wall.
6. Incision.
7. Diameter 183 cm.
8. Heisel (note 116).

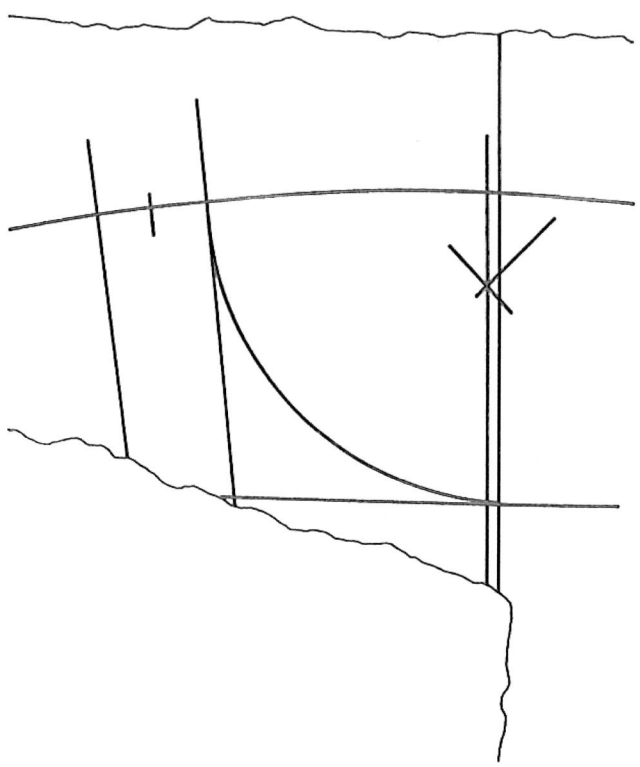

7.

1. Horizontal section of quarter of column.
2. The drawing represents a quarter of circle inscribed in a quadrangle. Two parallel segments probably show the extension of the flute.
3. Didyma, temple of Apollo, baseboard of the S wall of the adyton.
4. Around 250 BC.
5. Stone wall.
6. Incision.
7. 10, 97 x 83, 9 cm.
8. Heisel (note 117).

9. Catalogue of drawings of architectures in the Greek and Roman world

8.

1. Composition of rosette with a system of circles.
2. Seven circles are drawn: the center of the central circle is where the other six circles meet. With this way a rosette with six petals is obtained.
3. Didyma, temple of Apollo, baseboard of the adyton.
4. Around 250 BC.
5. Stone wall.
6. Drawing made with white colour on red ground.
7. Dimensions not given.
8. Haselberger (note 118).

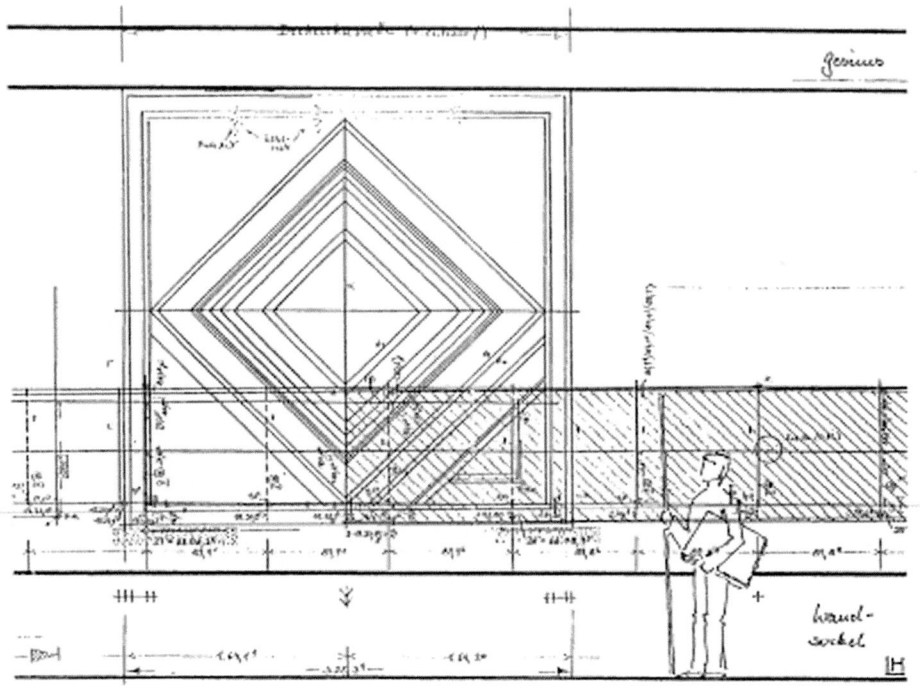

9.

1. Construction of panel of ceiling.
2. A grid of horizontal and vertical segments forms the shape of the panel. Four parallel segments mark, two at one side and two at the other, two parallel sides of a square panel. Lighter lines mark the concentric squares of the panel and two crossed segments divide the square in four compartments.
3. Didyma, temple of Apollo, baseboard of the N wall of the adyton.
4. Roman imperial times.
5. Stone wall.
6. Incision.
7. Dimensions not given.
8. Haselberger (note 119).

9. Catalogue of drawings of architectures in the Greek and Roman world

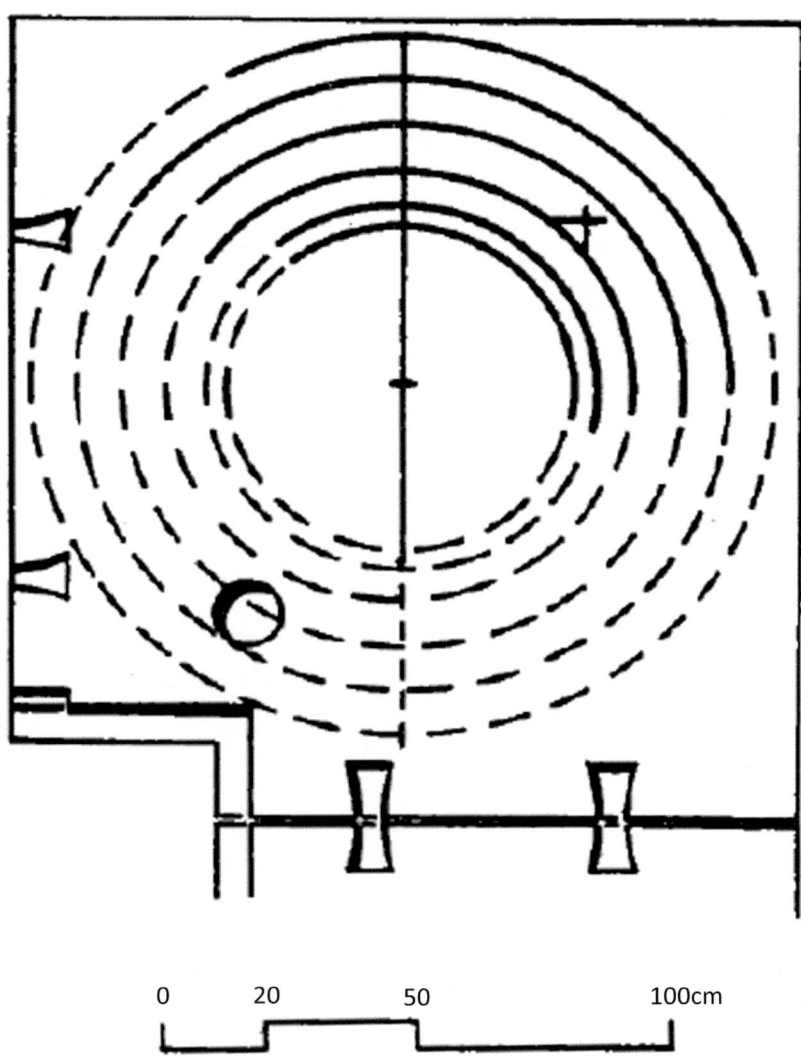

10.

1. Horizontal section of lower shaft.
2. Six concentric circles are drawn with indication of the diameter through a vertical line. The centre is also signed.
3. Iseum di Philae, eastern tower.
4. Around 100 BC.
5. Stone wall.
6. Incision.
7. Diameter 150 cm.
8. Heisel (note 121).

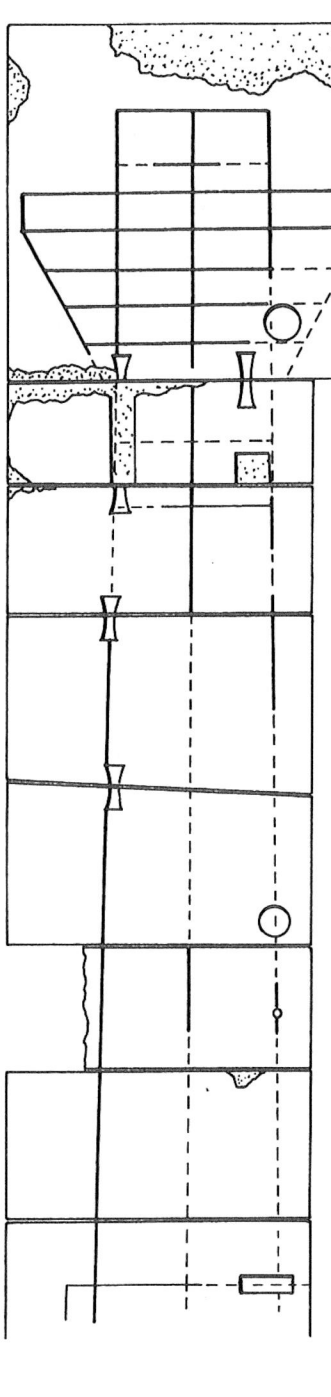

11.

1. Vertical section of column.
2. The axis and the two external vertical borders of the column are drawn. The tapering is shown. The capital is indicated through a scansion of five horizontal lines. The four lower lines are bordered at the sides by two oblique directrixes which show the upper enlargement of the capital. Above the fourth horizontal segment, the abacus is represented.
3. Iseum di Philae, eastern tower.
4. Around 100 BC.
5. Stone wall.
6. Incision.
7. 200 x 500 cm.
8. Heisel (note 122).

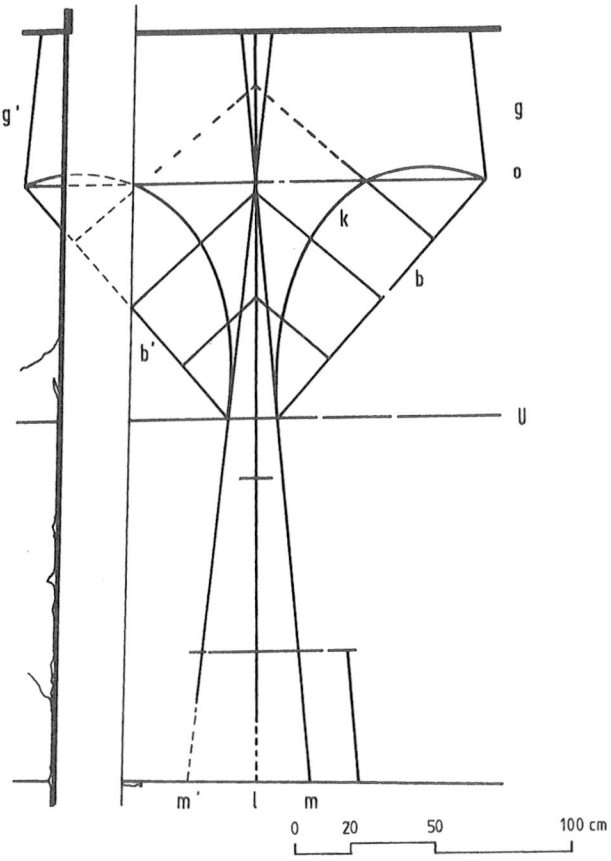

12.

1. Upper ending of flutes of a column.
2. The fillet between two flutes is shown with three segments: the central one indicates the axis of the fillet and the two lateral lines are oblique and convergent, indicating the vertical external borders of the fillet. The fillet is scanned by three horizontal segments. At the sides of the fillet, the upper ending of the two adjacent flutes is shown with two arcs of circle, of which the chords are also indicated. The two chords of circle, whose directions are oblique, are linked through three quadrangles. The upper ending of the upper shaft is shown by two parallel horizontal segments and by two vertical ones: the latter are slightly oblique and thus conform to the general tapering.
3. Western porticoed hall of the temple of Horus at Edfu.
4. Around 100 BC.
5. Floor slab.
6. Incision.
7. 182 x 271 cm.
8. Heisel (note 123).

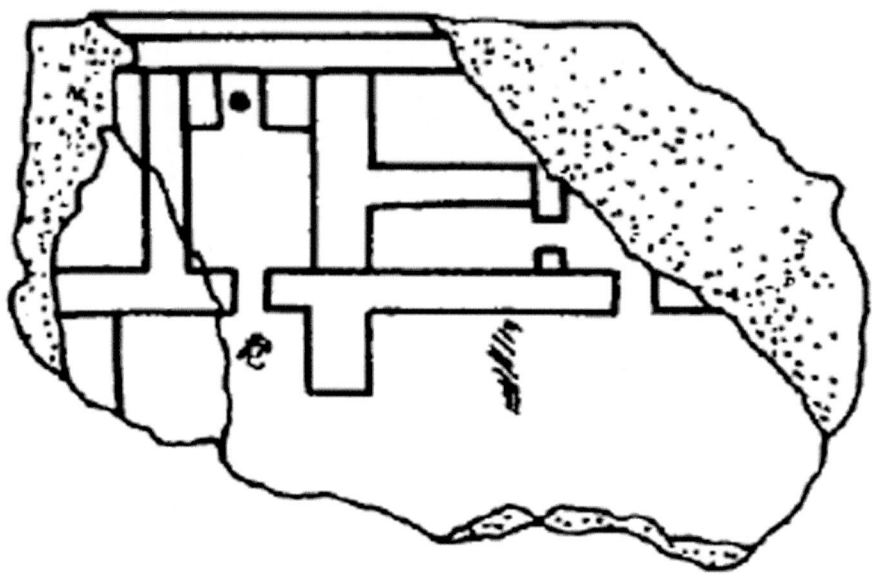

13.

1. Plan probably of a *forica*.
2. In the preserved fragment the plan of a building complex is represented: it includes four rectangle rooms and perhaps a central courtyard.
3. From Susa, Acropolis, at Paris, Louvre.
4. Seleucid age.
5. Clay tablet.
6. Incision.
7. Dimensions not given.
8. Heisel (note 125).

9. CATALOGUE OF DRAWINGS OF ARCHITECTURES IN THE GREEK AND ROMAN WORLD

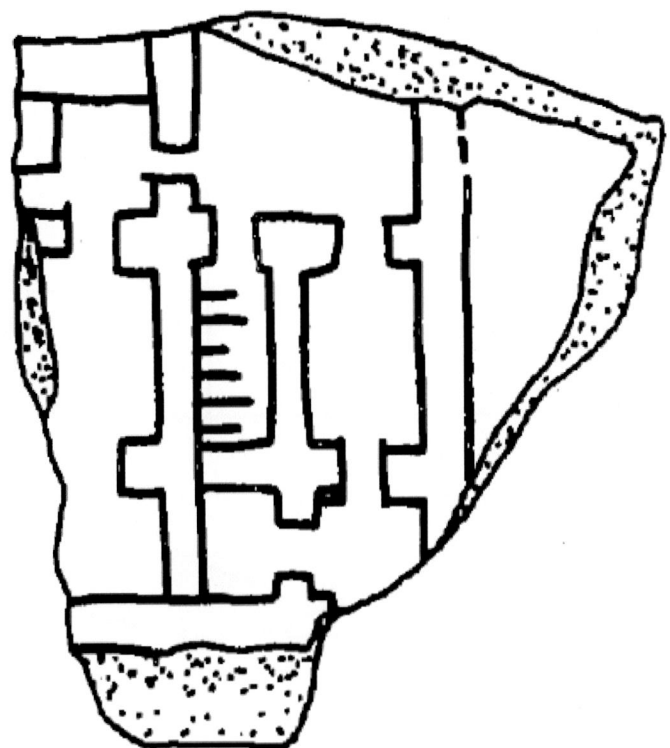

14.

1. Plan of architectural complex with ladder, perhaps to be identified with a section of the great Seleucid temple of Uruk.
2. The plan represents a building complex with three rectangle rooms and perhaps a courtyard: the room in the middle is interpreted as ladder.
3. From Susa, Acropolis, at Paris, Louvre.
4. Seleucid age.
5. Clay tablet.
6. Incision.
7. Dimensions not given.
8. Heisel (note 126).

68 DRAWINGS IN GREEK AND ROMAN ARCHITECTURE

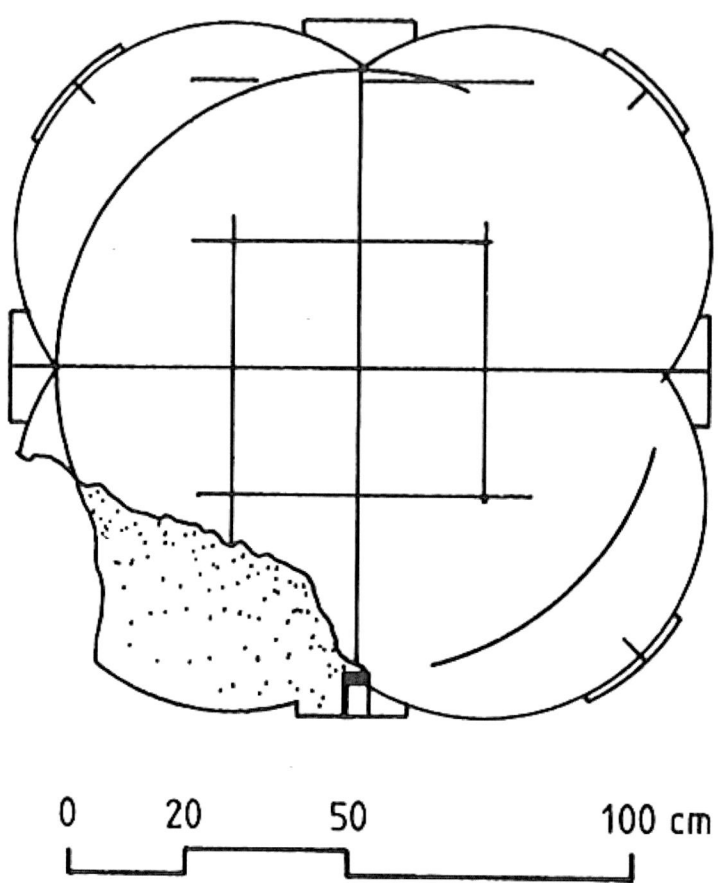

15.

1. 1. Lower face of capital.
2. 2. The drawing represents the lower face of a capital obtained with a circle divided in four quadrants by two crossed diameters. The central section of the circle is included in a square. An arc of circle is added to each quadrant. Rectangular projections are signed between the four arcs of circle.
3. 3. Nubia, Bab-al-Kalabsha, temple of Mandulis.
4. 4. About 30 BC.
5. 5. Unfinished stone capital.
6. 6. Incision.
7. 7. 124 x 124 cm.
8. 8. Heisel (note 127).

16.

1. Drawing of column.
2. The column is shown with its two external vertical lines, its upper shaft is delimited by two collars, decorated with vertical streaks, surmounted by a wreath of leafs and by a fan-shaped capital.
3. Nubia, Bab-al-Kalabsha, temple of Mandulis, on floor slab of the so called 'birth house' of the god.
4. Around 30 BC.
5. Stone floor
6. Incision.
7. 75 x 35 cm.
8. Heisel (note 128).

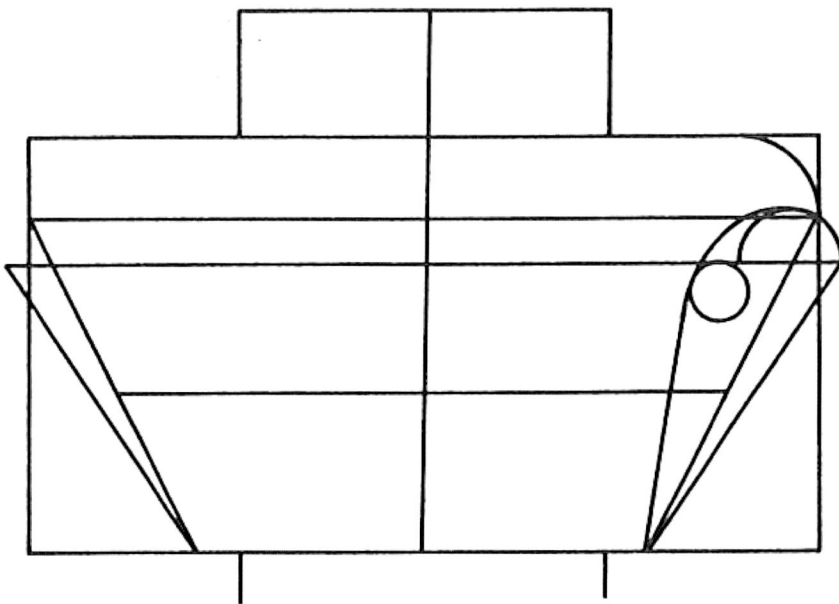

17.

1. Lotus capital.
2. The drawing is divided in two compartments by a vertical line which cuts a rectangle in two halves. The capital is obtained with two isosceles trapeziums, which overlap one the other. At the viewer's right side, the typical 'lotus leaf' of the capitals bearing this name is schematically represented.
3. Stone quarry of Gebel Abu Foda.
4. 1st century BC.
5. Stone.
6. Drawing with red colour.
7. 120 x 80 cm.
8. Heisel (note 129).

9. Catalogue of drawings of architectures in the Greek and Roman world

18.

1. Hator capital.
2. In an orthogonal grid a Hator capital is drawn. The front side of the capital appears in full prospect, but the side projections of the Hator heads are also shown.
3. Stone quarry of Gebel Abu Foda.
4. 1st century BC.
5. Stone.
6. Drawing with red colour.
7. 80 x 120 cm.
8. Heisel (note 130).

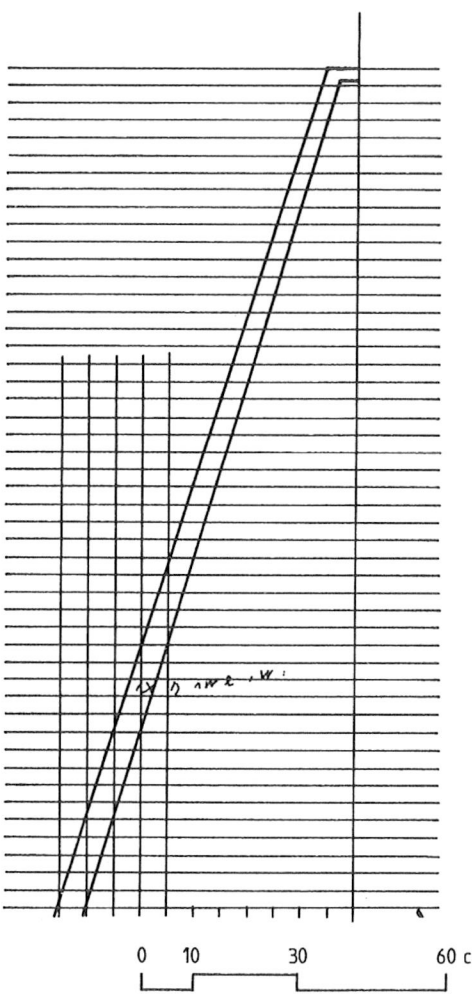

19.

1. Inclination of pyramid no. 2 of Meroe.
2. In a series of horizontal segments the inclination of the pyramid no. 2 of the northern group of pyramids of Meroe is drawn. Five vertical segments probably allow a more precise definition of the inclination. The vertical axis of the pyramid is also signed.
3. At Meidum, Mastaba no. 17.
4. 1st century BC.
5. Stone wall.
6. Incision.
7. 70 x 170 cm.
8. Heisel (note 131).

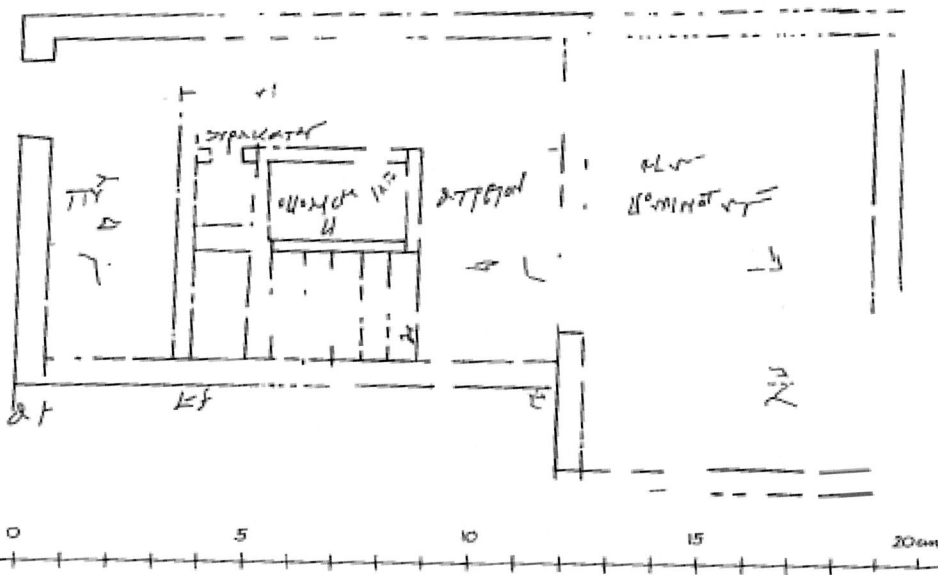

20.

1. Plan of house.
2. The house has its entrance from a short side. After the entrance there is a succession of three courtyards: the first is the entrance one, the second is the atrium and the third is a wide courtyard. The second courtyard gave access to a rectangular storeroom and to a room with *impluvium*. Numbers written inside these rooms probably gave their dimensions.
3. From Oxyrhynchus, *Oxyrhynchus Papyri* 24. 2406.
4. AD 2nd century.
5. Papyrus.
6. Ink drawing.
7. 22, 5 x 13 cm.
8. Haselberger and Settis (note 132).

74 DRAWINGS IN GREEK AND ROMAN ARCHITECTURE

P.Oxy. LXXI 4842

21.

1. Portico.
2. The upper sections of two Corinthian unfluted columns with their capitals are represented, as well as an architrave without fasciae but with upper taenia and a frieze with a decoration of shoots of acanthus.
3. From Oxyrhynchus, *Oxyrhynchus Papyri*, no. 71. 4842.
4. Around AD 140.
5. Papyrus.
6. Ink drawing.
7. 190 x 169 mm.
8. Coulton (note 133).

9. Catalogue of drawings of architectures in the Greek and Roman world

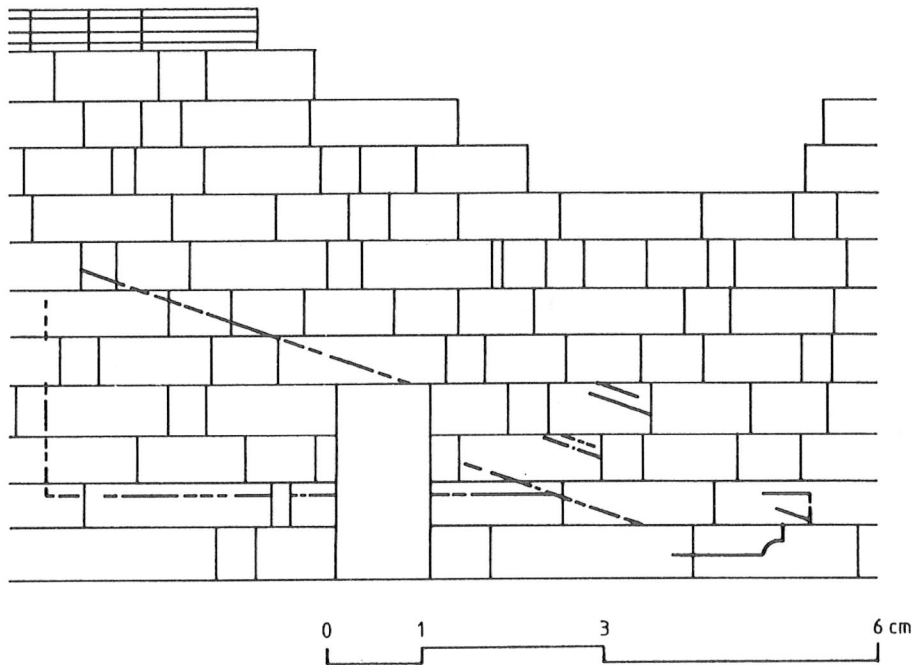

22.

1. Pediment of temple.
2. The half of the pediment of a temple is drawn with indication of the horizontal and oblique *simae*. A vertical line is signed from the top of the gable until the horizontal *sima*.
3. Lebanon, Bziza, Ionic temple.
4. Hadrianic–Antonine age.
5. Stone wall.
6. Incision.
7. 850 x 300 cm.
8. Heisel and Haselberger (note 134).

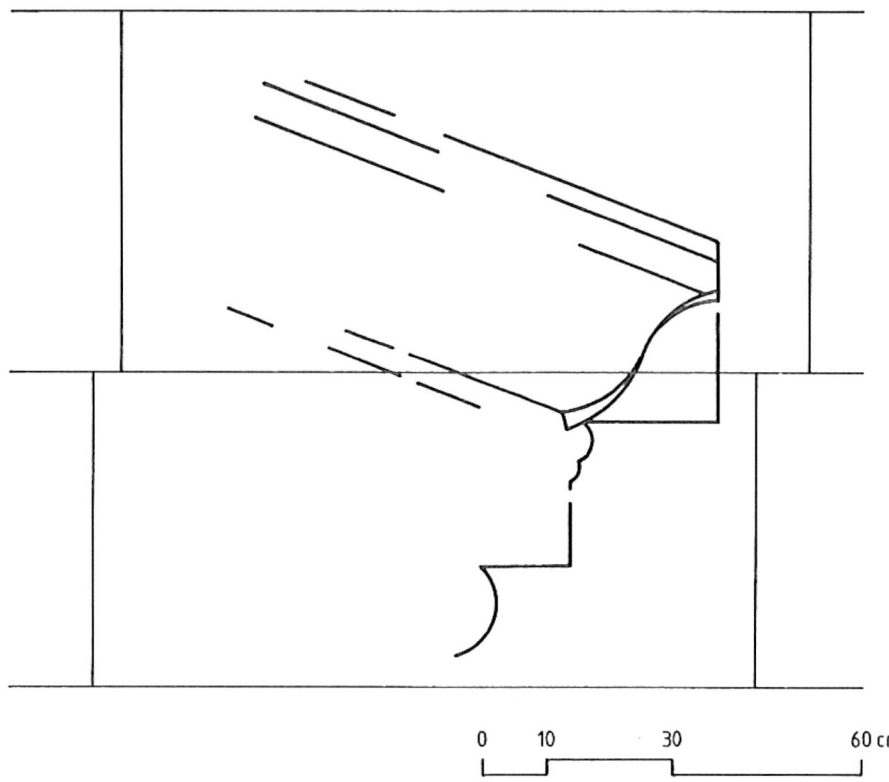

23.

1. Profile of entablature.
2. A profile of entablature is represented: the oblique sima, the geison and the lower mouldings are signed.
3. Lebanon, Bziza, Ionic temple.
4. Stone wall.
5. Hadrianic-Antonine age.
6. Incision.
7. 92 x 80 cm.
8. Heisel (note 135).

9. Catalogue of drawings of architectures in the Greek and Roman world

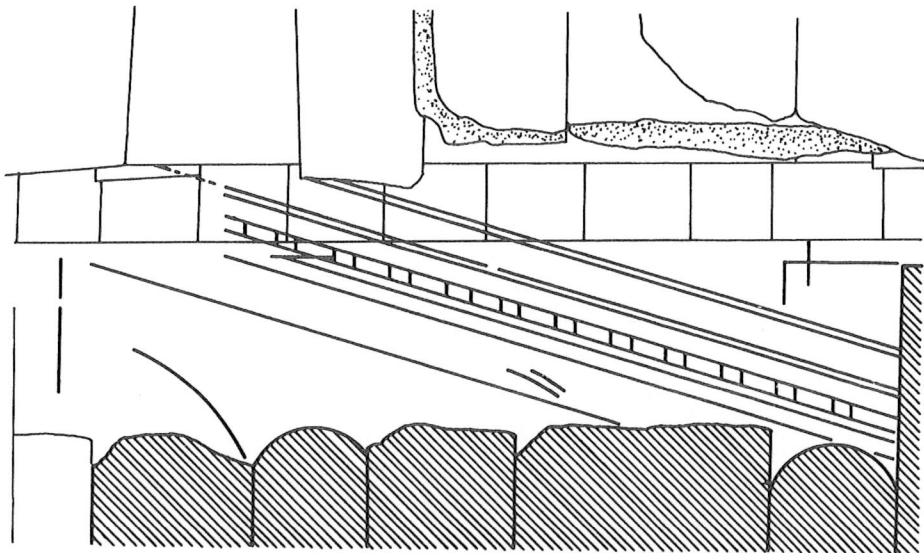

24.

1. Pediment
2. The oblique sima corresponding to the S section of the rear pediment of the temple of Jupiter at Baalbek is represented.
3. Baalbek, temple of Jupiter, platform of the temple, W side.
4. Julio-Claudian age.
5. Stone.
6. Incision.
7. 1200 x 400 cm.
8. Heisel (note 135).

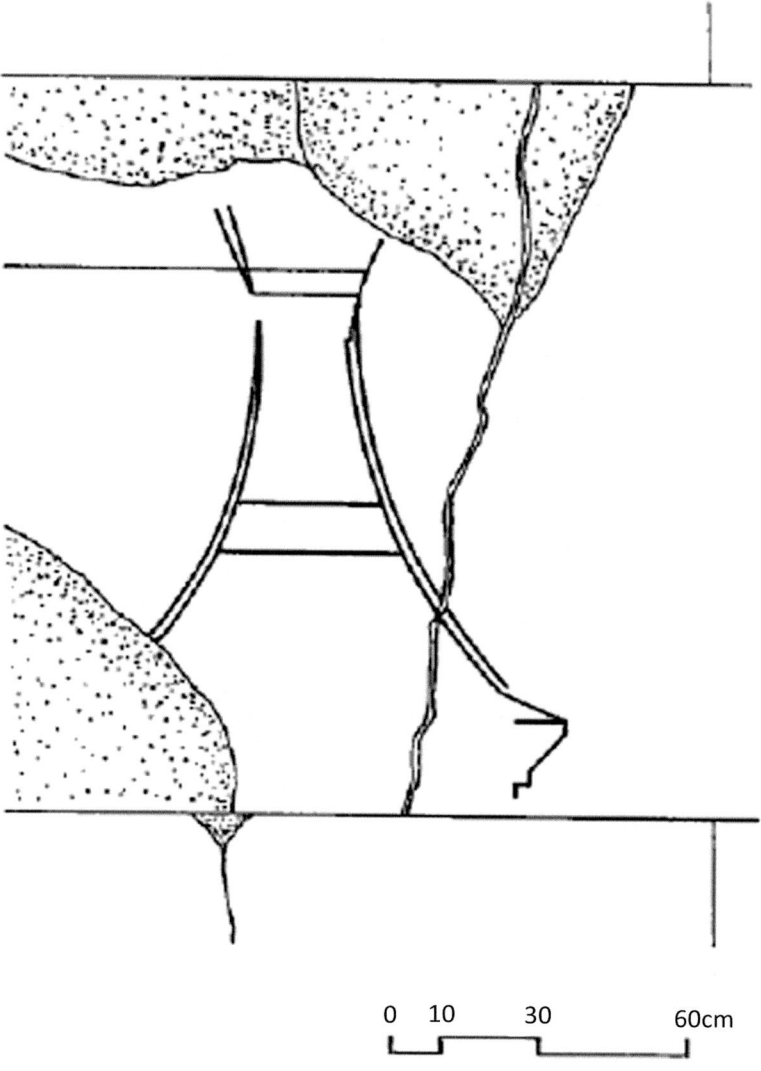

25.

1. Roof of fountain.
2. The drawing represents the vertical section of the entablature and of the concave roof of the fountain near the temple of Bacchus at Baalbek.
3. Baalbek, enclosing wall of the sanctuary of Jupiter, S side, in front of the N side of the temple of Bacchus.
4. Antonine age.
5. Stone.
6. Incision.
7. 1200 x 400 cm.
8. Heisel (note 136).

9. Catalogue of drawings of architectures in the Greek and Roman world

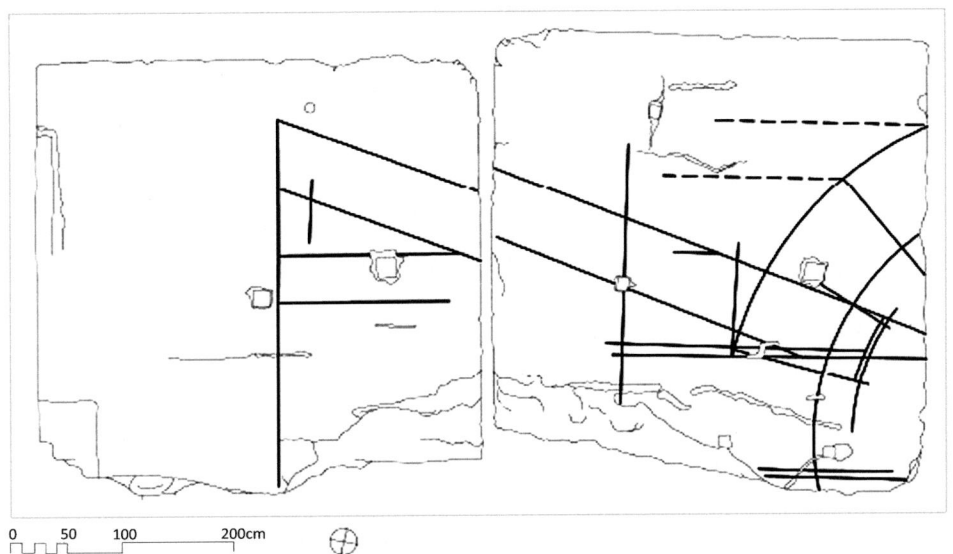

26 A.

1. Drawings of a triangle and of an arc of circle.
2. The drawing of the triangle bears an oblique band determined by two parallel lines, a horizontal line incised below that band, moreover three concentric arcs of circle are drawn in the area of the lower right corner of the triangle from the viewer's point of view. Perhaps it is the project of a floor decoration *opus sectile* with geometric patterns.
3. Baalbek, temple of Bacchus, stair leading to the entrance, N anta.
4. Antonine age.
5. Stone.
6. Incision.
7. 8 x 8 m.
8. Lohmann (note 138).

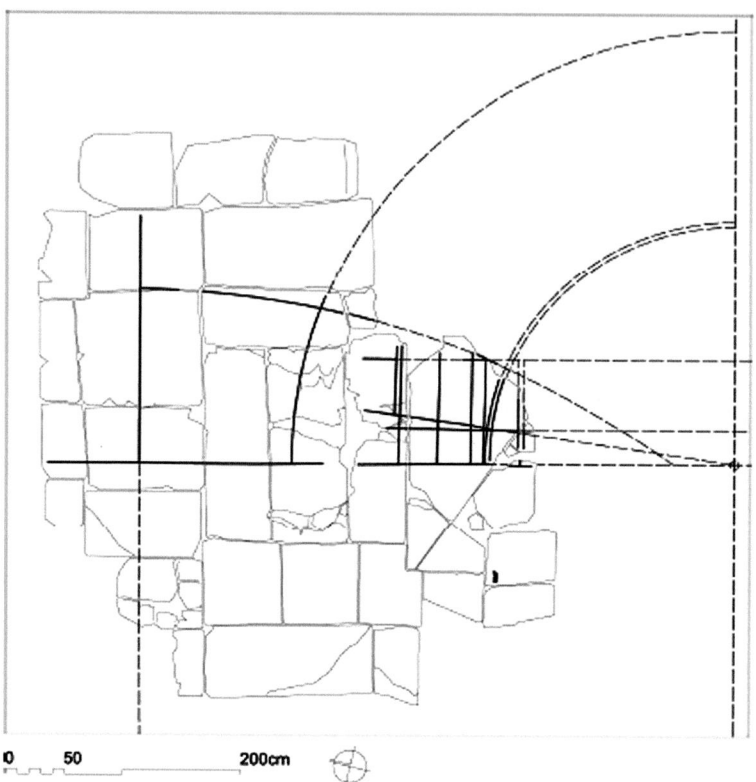

26 B.

1. Quarters and arc of circle.
2. Two concentric quarters of circle are represented and an arc of circle partly intersects the two quarters of circle. Parallel horizontal and vertical segments are incised in the area of the quarters of circle. An oblique segment may represent the curvature of the horizontal lines. Perhaps the orthogonal lines represent the portico of the *frons scaenae* in front of a cavea and of a semicircular orchestra. The arc of circle could mark the estension of the left parodos of the theatre. In that case, the smaller quarter of circle may represent the orchestra, while the section between the smaller and the larger circumference can be attributed to the cavea.
3. Baalbek, large courtyard between small altar and stair leading to the entrance of the temple of Jupiter.
4. Trajanic age.
5. Stone pavement.
6. Incision.
7. Around 5 m.
8. Lohmann (note 138).

9. Catalogue of drawings of architectures in the Greek and Roman world

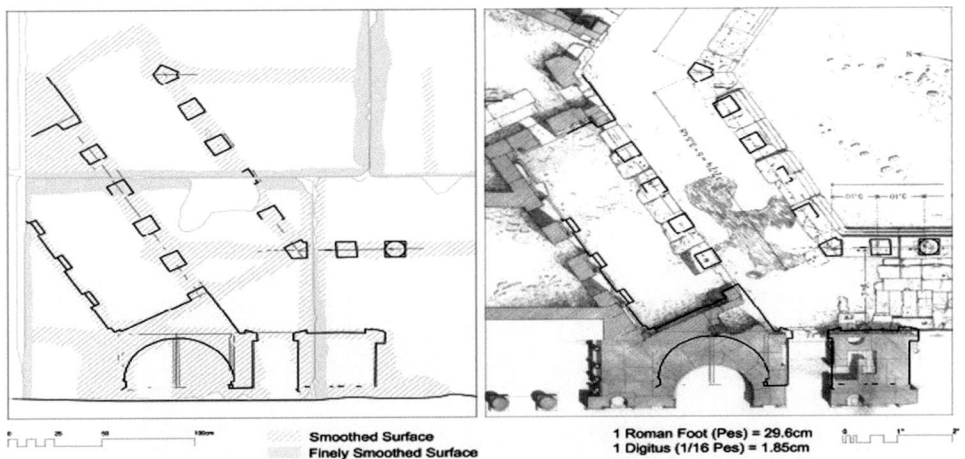

27.

1. Plan of the NW section of the exagonal courtyard of Baalbek.
2. The drawing represents the NW section of the so called exagonal courtyard of Baalbek. A rectangular exedra, the corner of an internal portico of the courtyard and a section of the same courtyard are represented. The buildings which border the courtyard in this corner are also signed.
3. Baalbek, sanctuary of Jupiter, N side, exedra.
4. Age of Philip the Arab.
5. Stone pavement.
6. Incision.
7. 4, 25 x 2, 60 cm.
8. Lohmann (note 138).

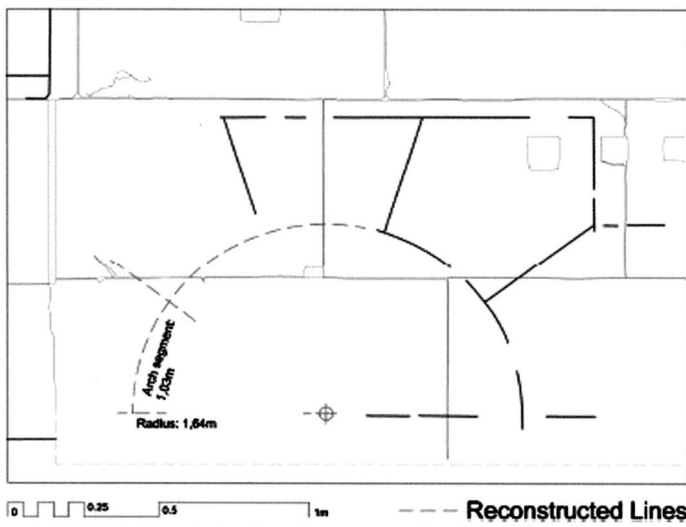

28.

1. Vault of exedra of the N side of the sanctuary of Jupiter at Baalbek.
2. The arch is represented with its barrel vault and with the *opus poligonale* above the barrel vault. The curve of the vault and the blocks of stone are clearly signed.
3. Baalbek, sanctuary of Jupiter, N side, exedra.
4. Age of Philip the Arab.
5. Stone pavement.
6. Incision.
7. Around 3 m.
8. Lohmann (note 138).

9. Catalogue of drawings of architectures in the Greek and Roman world

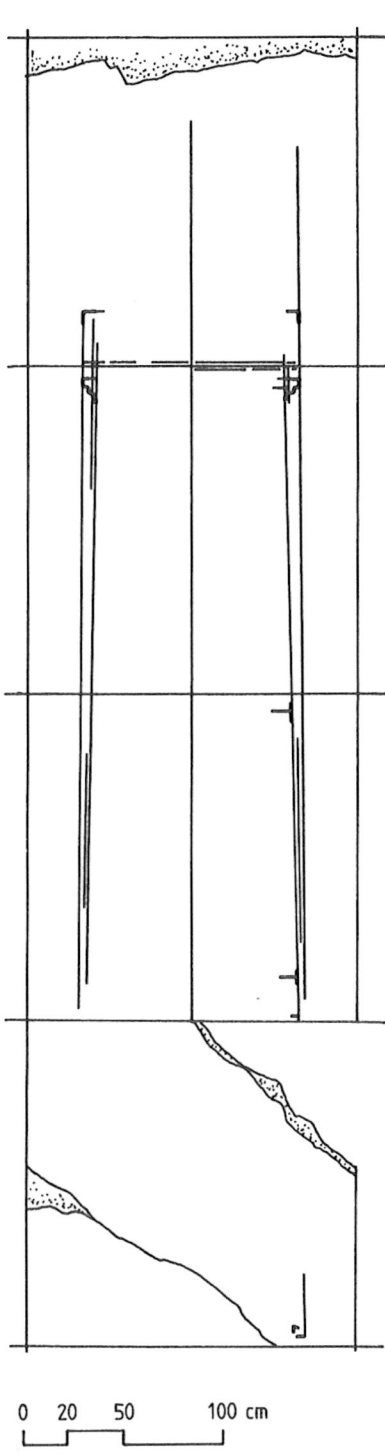

29.

1. Vertical section of shaft of column.
2. The vertical axis of the column, the vertical external directrixes and the diagonals of the tapering are signed: perhaps a shaft of column of the Ionic temple of the terrace of the theatre of Pergamum in its Hellenistic phase is represented as reminder for the reconstruction of the building in AD 2nd century.
3. Pergamum, terrace of the theatre, Ionic temple, baseboard of the E wall of the temple.
4. AD 2nd century.
5. Stone wall
6. Incision.
7. 120 x 630 cm.
8. Heisel (note 139).

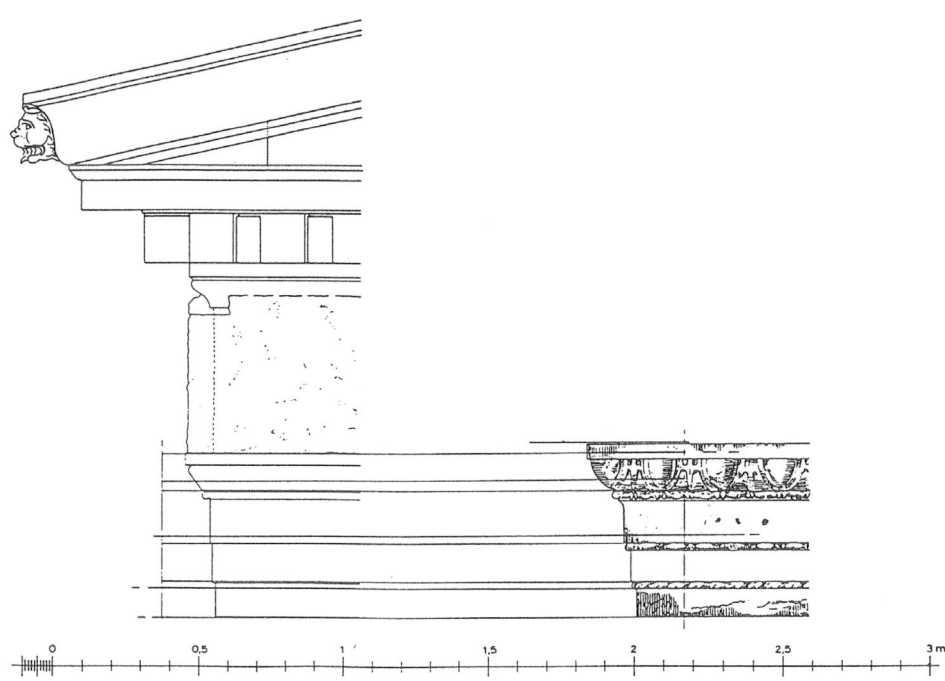

30.

1. Left corner of the entablature of the facade of the Ionic temple on the terrace of the theatre at Pergamum.
2. Horizontal and vertical lines give the height of the elements which compose the entablature of the front of the Ionic temple on the terrace of the theatre of Pergamum.
3. Pergamum, terrace of the theatre, Ionic temple, W wall of the temple.
4. AD 2nd century.
5. Stone wall.
6. Incision.
7. Around 2, 5 m.
8. Haselberger (note 140).

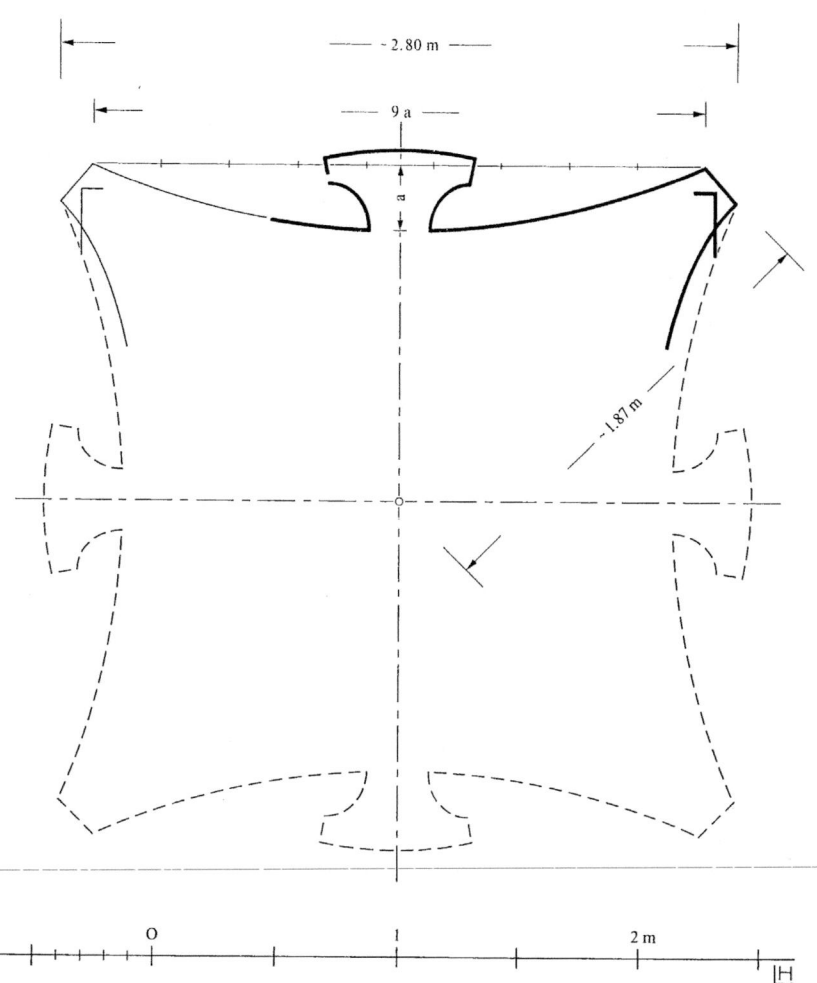

31.

1. Abacus of Corinthian capital of pillar.
2. The line of a short side of the abacus of a Corinthian capital of pillar is incised: the concave directrix of the short side, the central projection, the projection between the short side and the adjacent long side and the curved stretch of the latter are specified.
3. Rome, area S of the Mausoleum of Augustus.
4. Hadrianic age, by analogy with the drawing no. 32 which has a very similar craftsmanship.
5. Stone pavement.
6. Incision.
7. Around 2 m.
8. Haselberger (note 141).

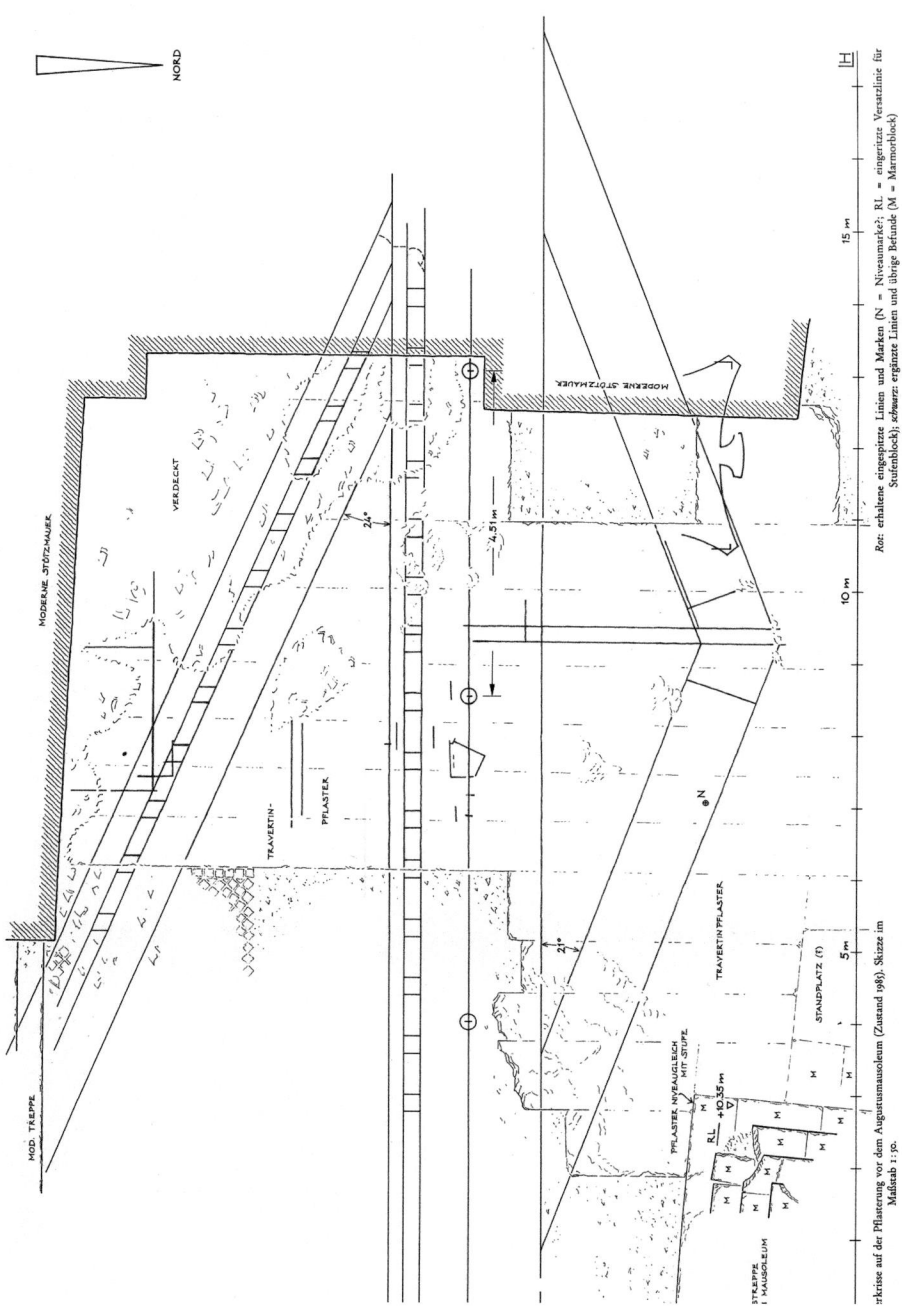

32.

9. CATALOGUE OF DRAWINGS OF ARCHITECTURES IN THE GREEK AND ROMAN WORLD 87

32.

1. Pediment and right angle entablature of the pronaos of the Hadrianic Pantheon.
2. The right angle of the pediment, with indication of the height of the oblique and horizontal *simae*, of the dentil, of the cornice and of the frieze, is represented. At N of this drawing, the central section of the pediment, with indication of the oblique *simae* and of the vertical axis of the pediment are also signed.
3. Roma, area S of the Mausoleum of Augustus.
4. Hadrianic period.
5. Stone pavement.
6. Incision.
7. Around 9 x 8 m.
8. Haselberger (note 141).

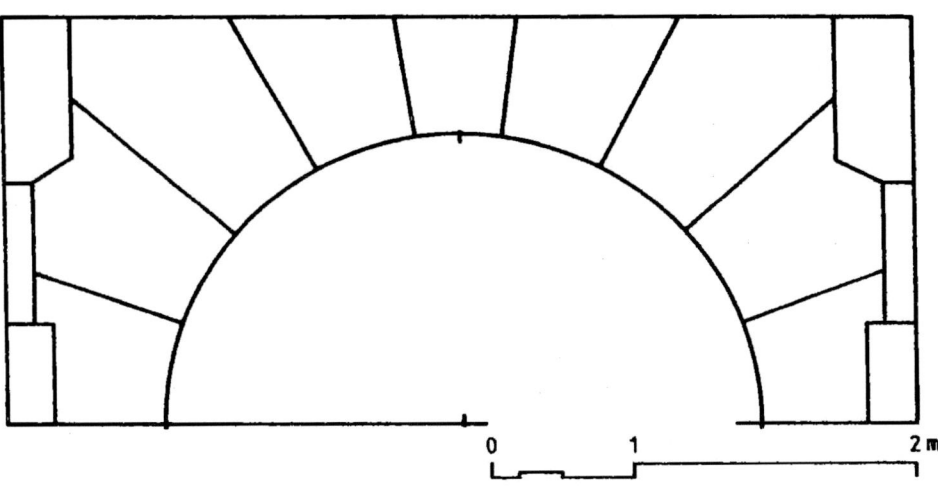

33.

1. Drawing of an arch.
2. A semicircular arch is represented, with indication of the *opus poligonale* above the arch. Probably it represents one of the arcades of the inferior external order of the amphitheater.
3. Ancient Capua, today Santa Maria di Capua Vetere, large anphitheater (so called Campanian anphitheater), pavement.
4. Hadrianic-Antonine age.
5. Stone pavement.
6. Incision.
7. 650 x 300 cm.
8. Heisel (note 142).

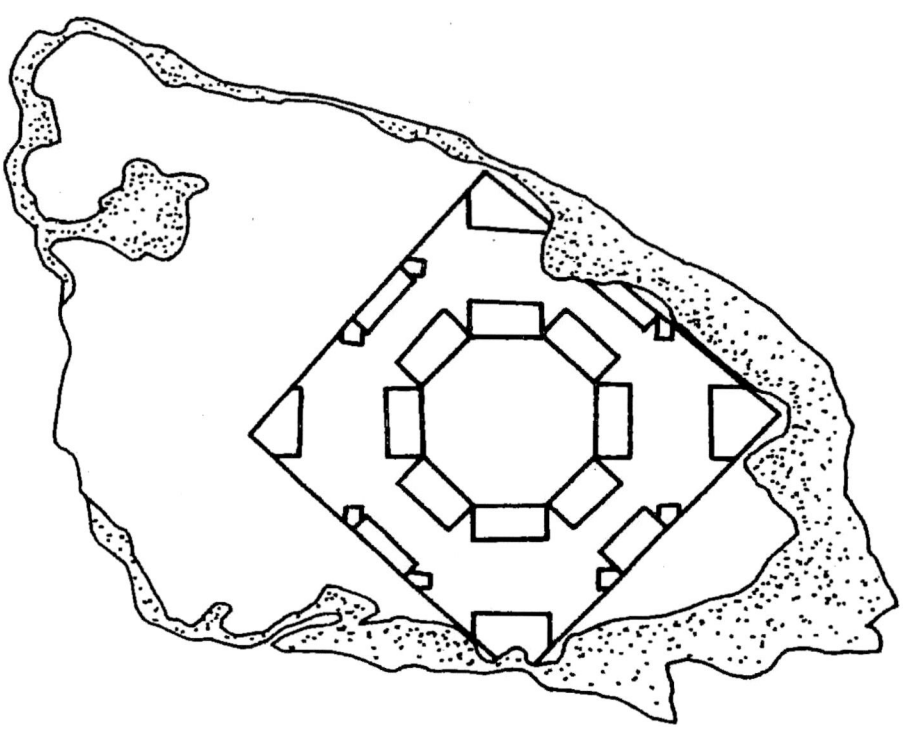

34.

1. Rosette.
2. A rosette is made with an octagon. A rectangle is drawn on each side of this geometric figure. That pattern is at the centre of a square: along the perimeter of this figure quadrangular patterns are also represented. Perhaps it was part of the decorative display of the amphitheater.
3. Ancient Capua, today Santa Maria di Capua Vetere, large anphitheater (so called Campanian amphitheater), on one of the pillars with semicolumns supporting the arcade of the external inferior order.
4. Hadrianic-Antonine age.
5. Stone block.
6. Incision.
7. 140 x 107 cm.
8. Heisel (note 143).

9. Catalogue of drawings of architectures in the Greek and Roman world

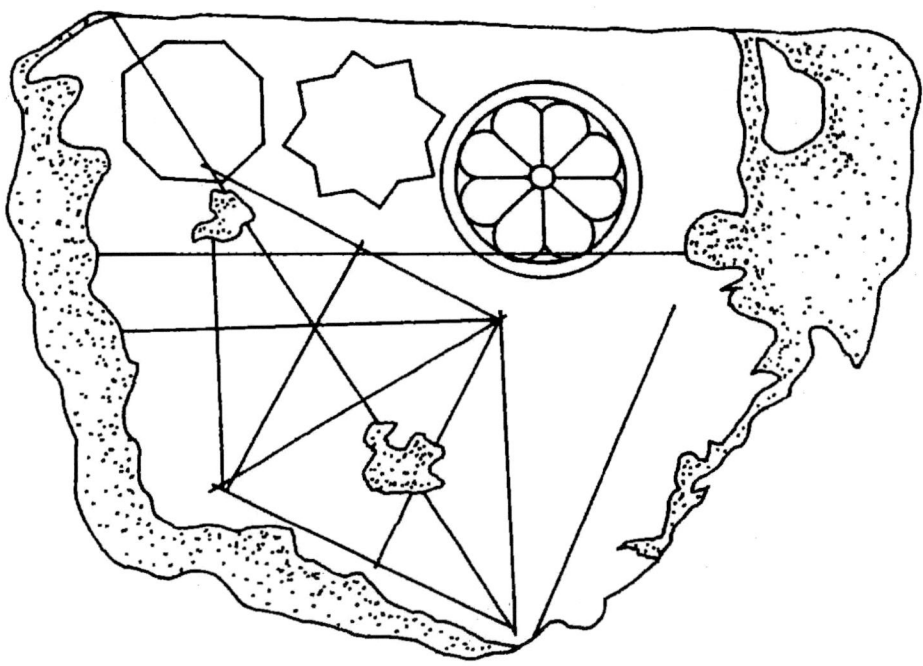

35.

1. Geometric patterns.
2. Four geometric patterns are drawn: an octagon, a polyhedron composed of two squares, a rosette with circular eye, eighth petals and inscribed in two circumferences, and an isosceles rhombus endowed with segments connecting the angles and the middle of the sides. Perhaps part of the decorative display of the amphitheater.
3. See no. 34.
4. See no. 34.
5. See no. 34.
6. See no. 34.
7. 170 x 105 cm.
8. See no. 34.

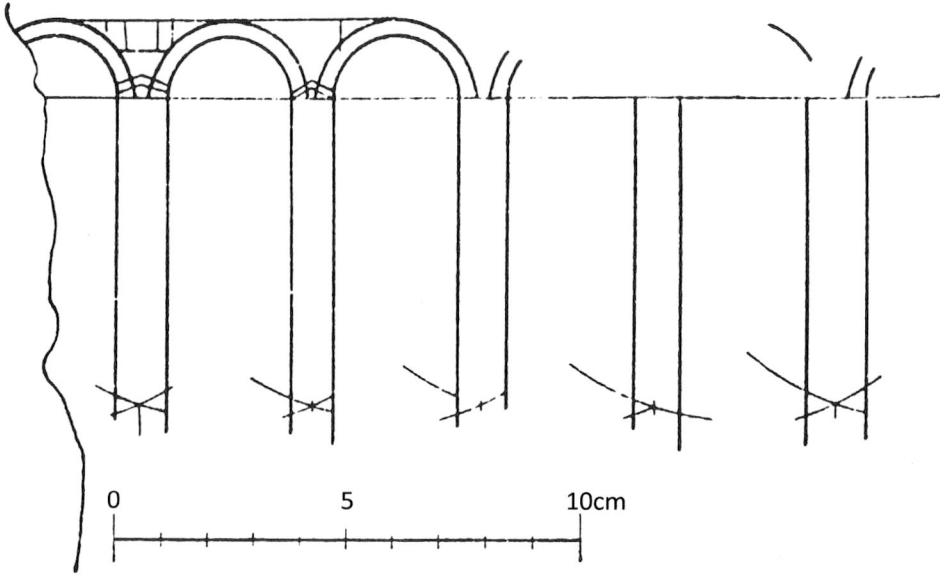

36.

1. Sequence of inferior external arcade of an amphitheater.
2. An arcade with indication of six semicircular arches, of the pillars which support them and of the walls supported by them is drawn: probably it represents a section of the inferior external arcade of the amphitheater.
3. Pola, amphitheater, third pillar W of the main entrance to the monument, baseboard.
4. Probably Vespasianic period
5. Stone block.
6. Incision.
7. 17 cm of length.
8. Haselberger (note 144).

9. Catalogue of drawings of architectures in the Greek and Roman world

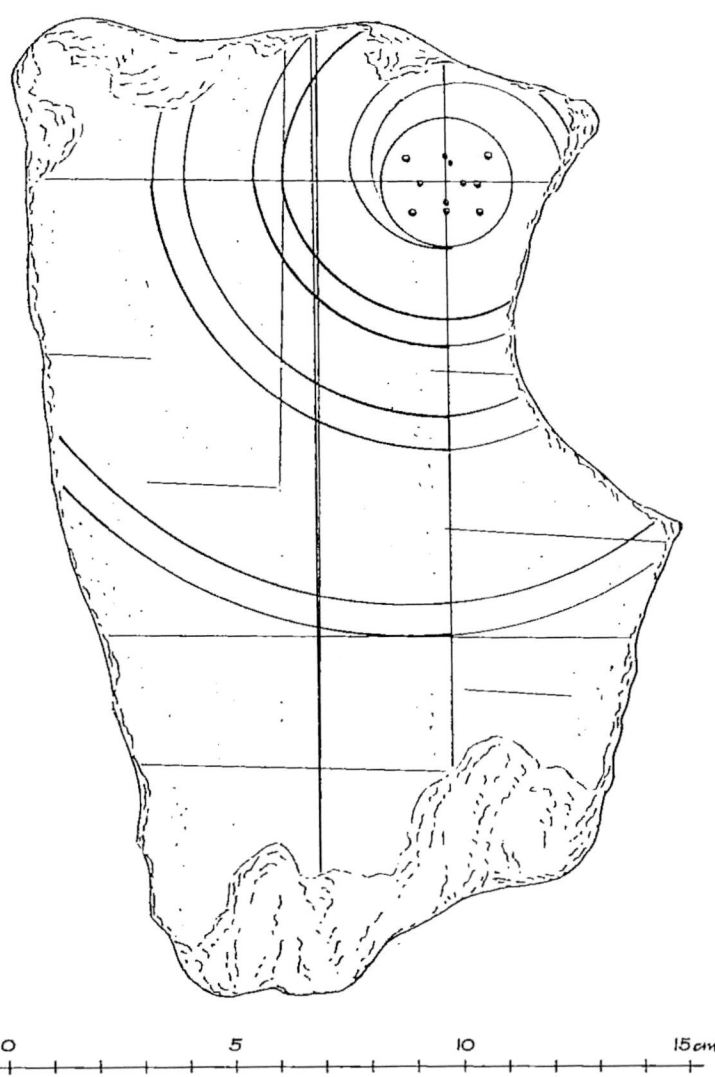

37.

1. Volute of Ionic capital.
2. A volute of Ionic capital is represented, with indication of the eye, the volute being indicated with two curved lines at unvaried distance.
3. From Thysdrus, at Bern, Museum of the Seminar of Classical Archaeology.
4. AD 2nd century.
5. Marble slab, probably mobile marble panel used in order to make volutes.
6. Incision.
7. 13, 2 x 21, 8 cm.
8. Loertscher, Heisel and Haselberger (note 145).

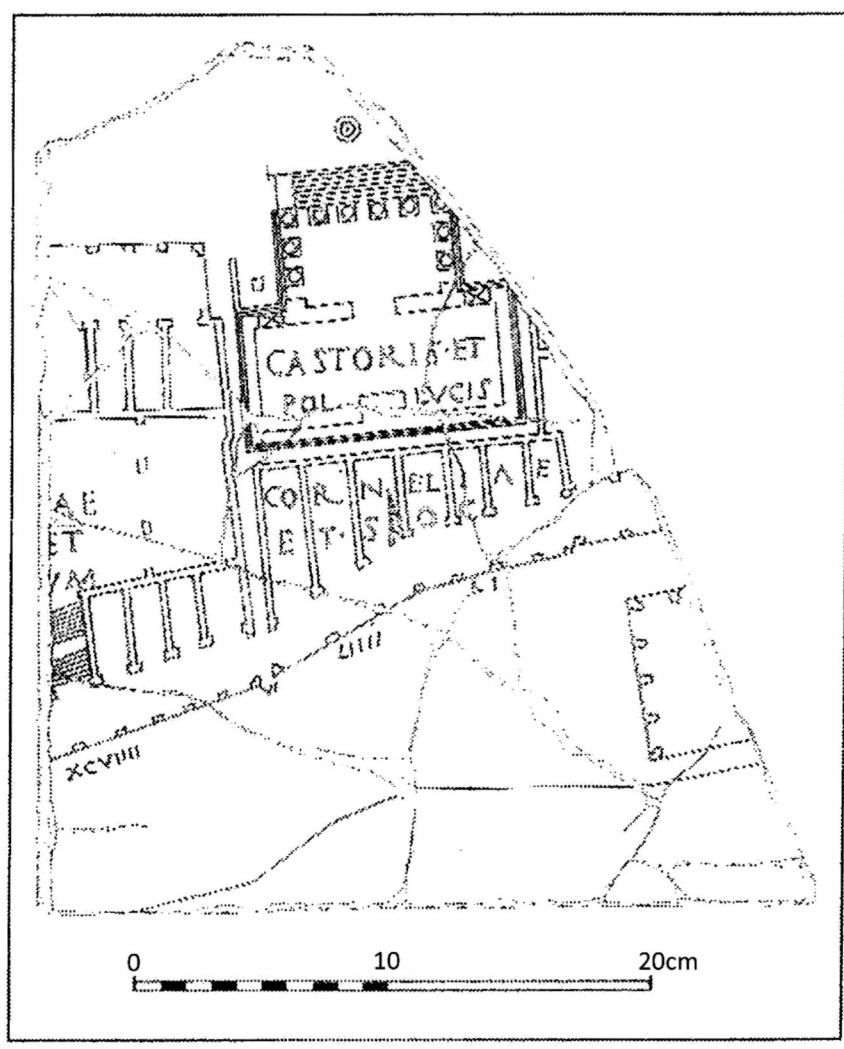

38.

1. Plan of the temple of the Dioscuri in the Circus Flaminius at Rome.
2. The temple of the Dioscuri *in Circo Flaminio* is represented: hexastyle, with transverse cell and round altar in front of the entrance stair. Few *horrea* and a porched road opened to the Tiber are also incised.
3. Found at Rome, in Trastevere, in Via Anicia, now in the Lapidarium of the Roman National Museum.
4. AD 1st century.
5. Slab of Luna marble.
6. Incision.
7. 30 x 29, 7 cm.
8. Tucci (note 148).

9. CATALOGUE OF DRAWINGS OF ARCHITECTURES IN THE GREEK AND ROMAN WORLD

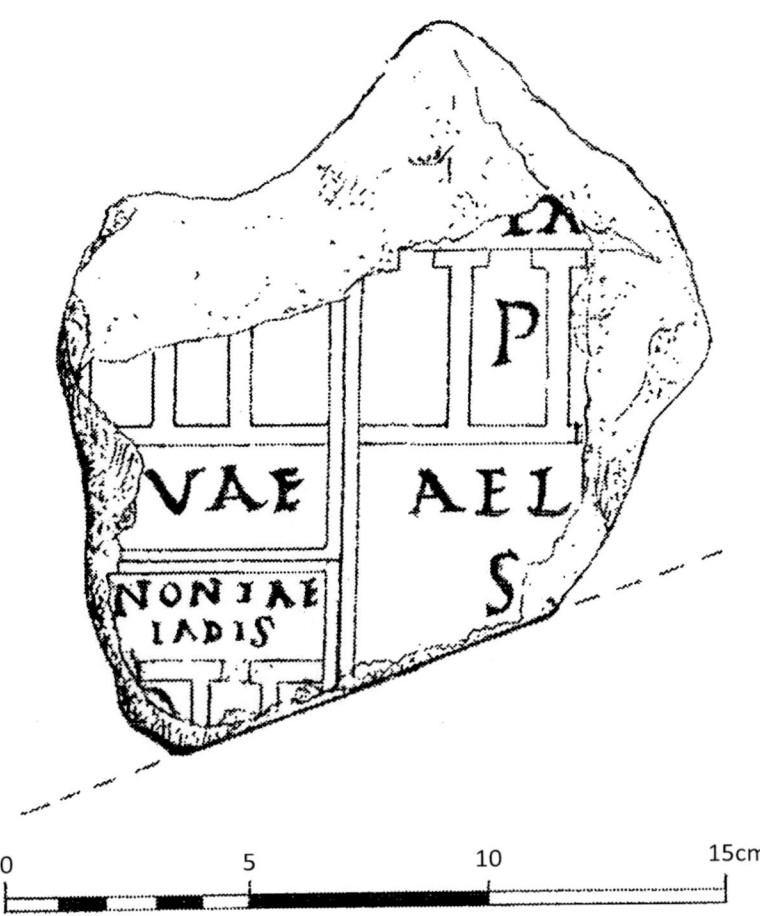

39.

1. Plan with *tabernae* and *horrea*
2. The plan shows from above a line of six rooms, probably *tabernae*, open to a road and separated by a double wall. Below the *tabernae*, there are two inner rooms, perhaps courtyards, separated by double walls. Below these courtyards, there are other rooms, perhaps storerooms.
3. Found at Rome, in Via della Polveriera, near Via Labicana, now in the Museo della Civilta' Romana.
4. Flavian age?
5. Upholstery slab in Proconnesian marble (perhaps pertinent to the near Baths of Titus).
6. Incision.
7. 12, 4 x 13, 7 cm.
8. Meneghini and Santangeli Valenzani (note 148) 27-28.

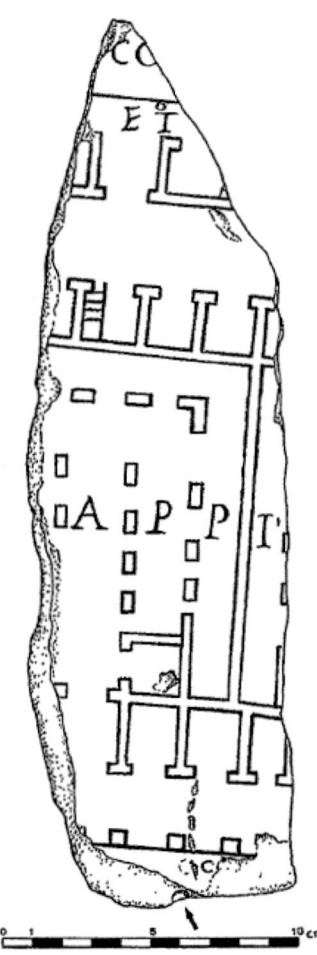

40.

1. Plan with *tabernae*.
2. A complex of buildings with fronts of *tabernae* at both the inferior and superior sides is represented. A large hypostyle room is placed at the centre of the fragment. The *tabernae* of the inferior section of the fragment open to a portico with pillars.
3. Found at Rome in the Forum of Nerva, now in the Ufficio Fori Imperiali of the Soprintendenza BBCC of the Comune di Roma.
4. End of AD 1st century.
5. Slab in Luna marble, perhaps destined to the pavement of the square of the Forum of Nerva.
6. Incision.
7. 30, 5 x 9 cm.
8. Meneghini and Santangeli Valenzani (note 148) 28-29 and 197-200.

9. Catalogue of drawings of architectures in the Greek and Roman world

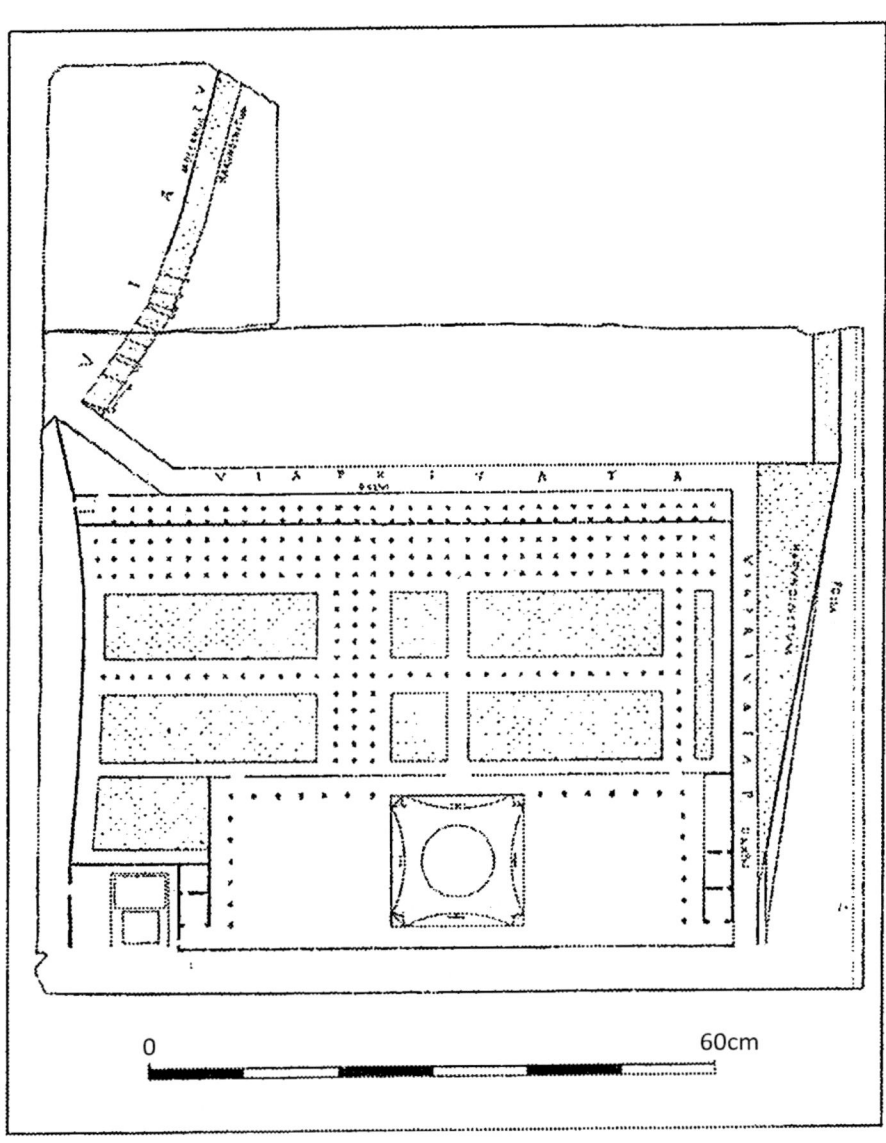

41.

41.

1. Plan of mausoleum with garden.
2. The plan represents a mausoleum with garden. The entrance from a public road is shown. Moreover the private road which allowed the access to the tomb and bordered its rectangular plan on two sides is signed. The private road splits the funerary area from a field of reeds, which is indicated with the word *harundinetum*, beyond which there is a canal, indicated with the word *fossa*. The graveyard is divided between a grove, where eighth rectangular areas may be identified as flower beds, and the funerary area, which has a mausoleum in the middle: the latter building bears a square podium and a square central body with concave sides supported by a rotunda. At the sides of the mausoleum, lines of trees are disposed in a double L configuration. Service buildings are found at the two sides.
3. Rom, Christian cemetery of the SS. Marcellinus and Petrus in Via Labicana, later in the Fabretti collection, finally in the Lapidario of the Palazzo Ducale at Urbino.
4. AD 1st century.
5. Marble slab.
6. Incision.
7. 89 x 71 cm.
8. Meneghini and Santangeli Valenzani (note 148) 30 -31.

42.

Restitution drawing of the Mausoleum in the plan no. 41. From C. Huelsen, 'Piante icnografiche incise in marmo', *RM* 5 (1890) 46-63, particularly 56, fig. 5.

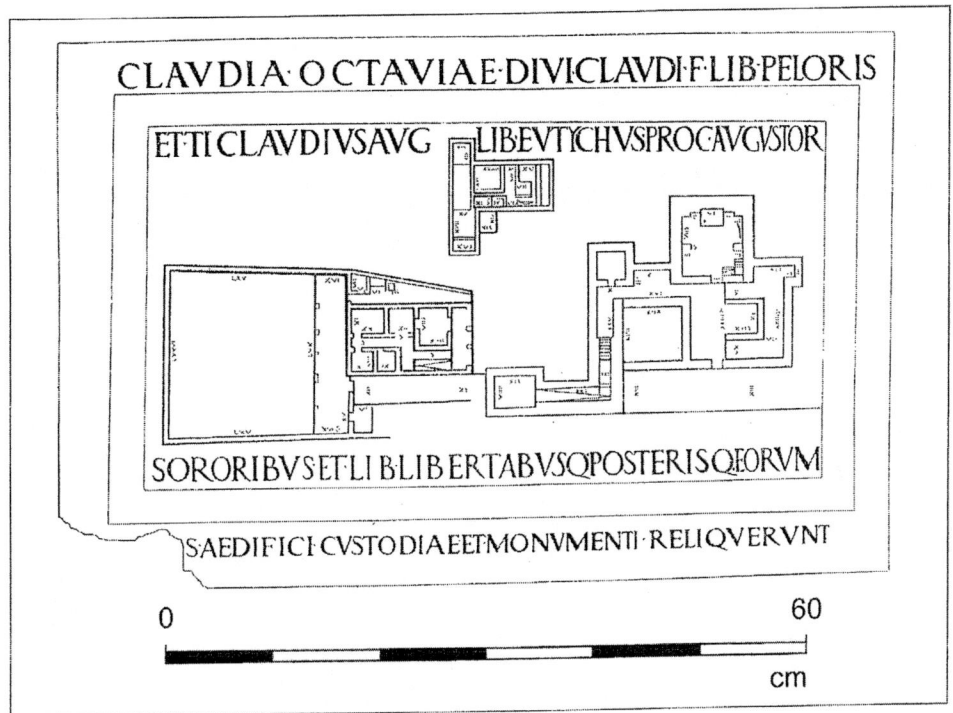

43.

1. Plan of a small funerary temple with house of keepers.
2. The map represents three plans: at the left the ground floor of the *aedificium custodiae* is represented: as it is specified in the inscription, it was destined to the house of keepers and endowed with an adjacent garden. At the centre above there is the plan of the second floor. At the right there is the *monumentum*, i. e. the monumental tomb, which was endowed with a small rectangular funerary temple with courtyard in front and other spaces at the sides. The plan was accompanied by the dedicatory inscription of two freedmen.
3. Rome, ramparts of the Belvedere, later Gaddi collection at Florence, then Oddi collection at Perugia, finally Perugia, Museo Archeologico.
4. Between AD 54 and 61 for prosopographic reasons.
5. Cladding slab in Luna marble, perhaps placed on the enclosing wall or on the tomb.
6. Incision.
7. 50 x 82 cm.
8. Meneghini and Santangeli Valenzani (note 148) 31-34.

44.

Restitution drawing of the tomb in the plan no. 43.
From Huelsen (see cat. no. 42) 49, fig. 1.

9. Catalogue of drawings of architectures in the Greek and Roman world

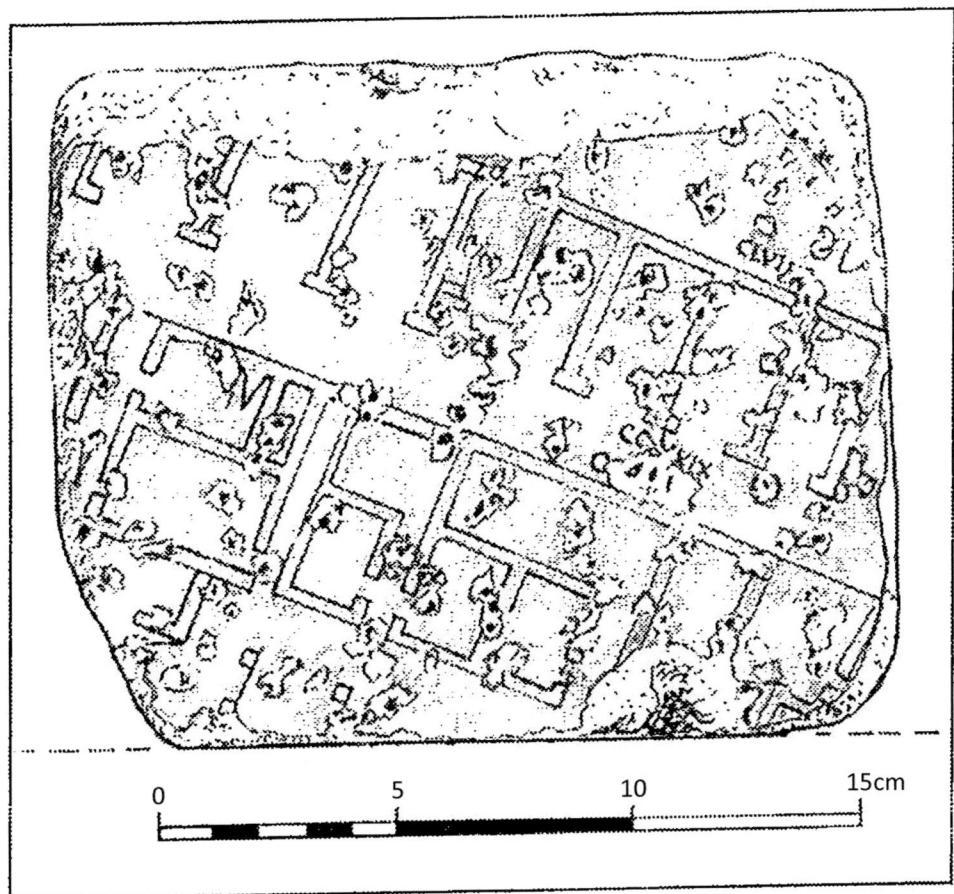

45.

1. Plan with *horrea* and *tabernae*.
2. The plan represents a series of rooms opened to a road. At the other side of the road there is a double line of rooms which are opened to an unroofed area, with a portico of pillars.
3. Found at Portus, near the *Insula Sacra*, in the tomb no. 107, which was inserted in the tomb of Julia Procula (no. 106) of Trajanic period. Perhaps the plan was deposed in the tomb as document celebrating the property of the deceased.
4. Trajanic age?
5. Slab of Luna marble.
6. Incision.
7. 18, 2 x 15, 1 cm.
8. Meneghini and Santangeli Valenzani (note 148) 34-35.

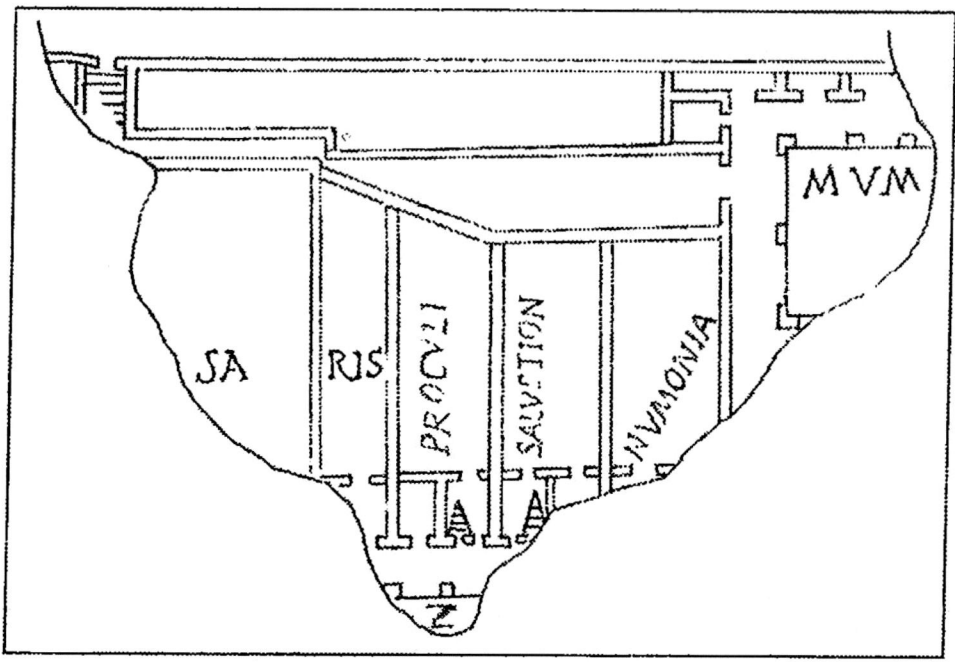

46.

1. Plan of rooms for business.
2. The plan represents from above a long wall, perhaps the embankment of a river, provided with stair (toward the river?), then a courtyard with a portico of pillars. Finally *horrea* or *tabernae* open to a portico. Probably it represents a stretch of the ancient topography of Rome along the Tiber.
3. The plan stood at Amelia in the Church of S. Secundus and its whereabouts are not known. It had been copied by C. Brancatelli, *Antiquae Amerinorum lapidum inscriptions*, Biblioteca Ambrosiana di Milano, folium 29.
4. Since the plan is lost, the date cannot be determined.
5. Probably on marble slab.
6. Incision.
7. Since the plan was lost, the dimensions cannot be determined.
8. Meneghini and Santangeli Valenzani (note 148) 35-36.

9. Catalogue of drawings of architectures in the Greek and Roman world

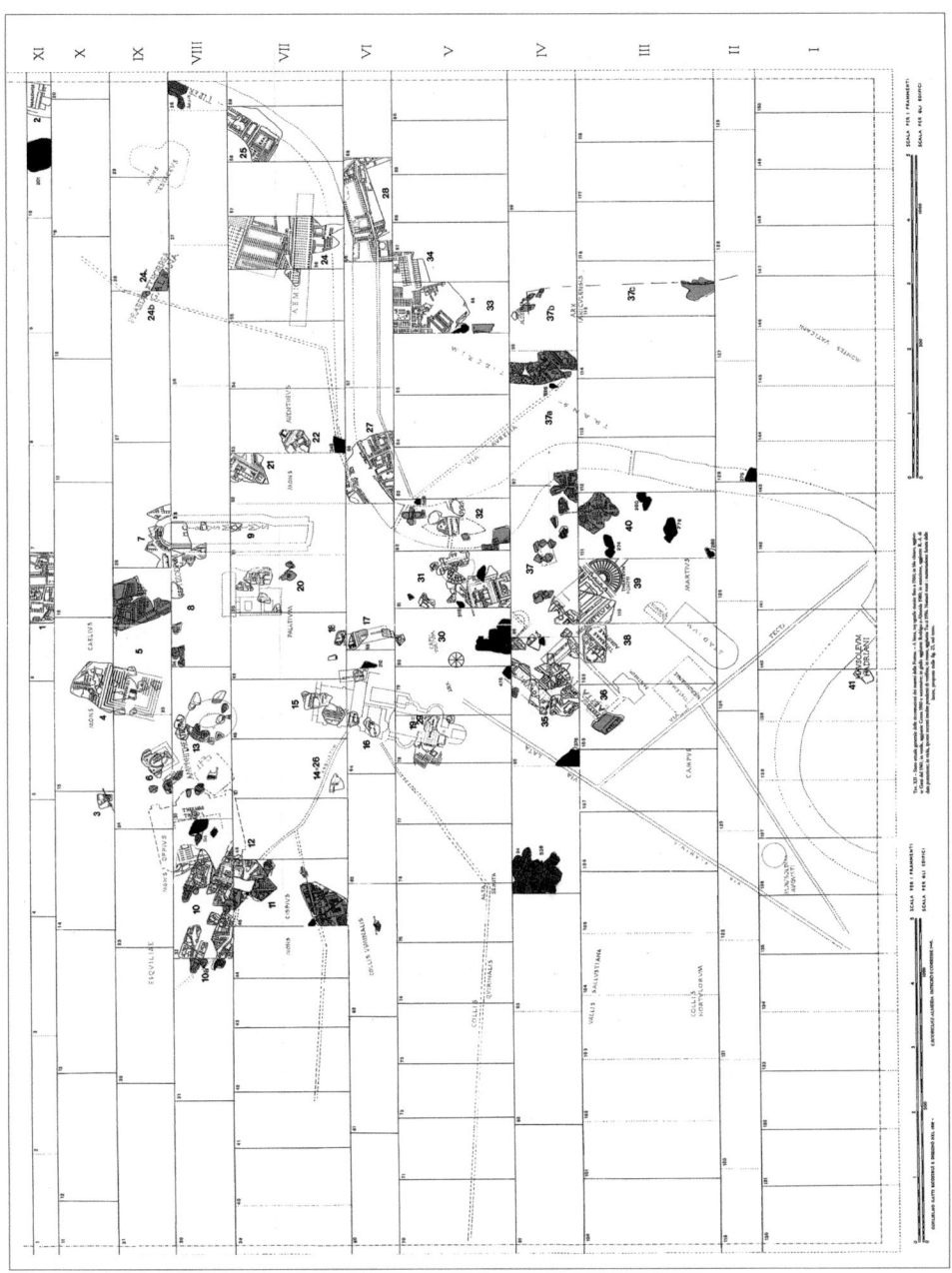

47.

1. Representation of the city of Rome (*Forma Urbis Romae*).
2. The whole city of Rome was represented with this map, with schematic representations of the plans of the most important buildings which composed the urban fabric. 1200 fragments of this map have been found.
3. Originally the map was exposed at Rome, in the W room of the *templum Pacis*. Now the surviving fragments are kept at Rome, in the Museum of the Roman Civilization.
4. AD 203-211.
5. Rectangular support in Luna marble.
6. Incision.
7. Around 18, 22 x 13 m.
8. Meneghini and Santangeli Valenzani (note 148) 41-156 and E. D'Ambrosio *et alii,* 'Nuovi frammenti di piante marmoree dagli scavi dell'aula di culto del templum Pacis', *BullComm* 112 (2011) 67-76.

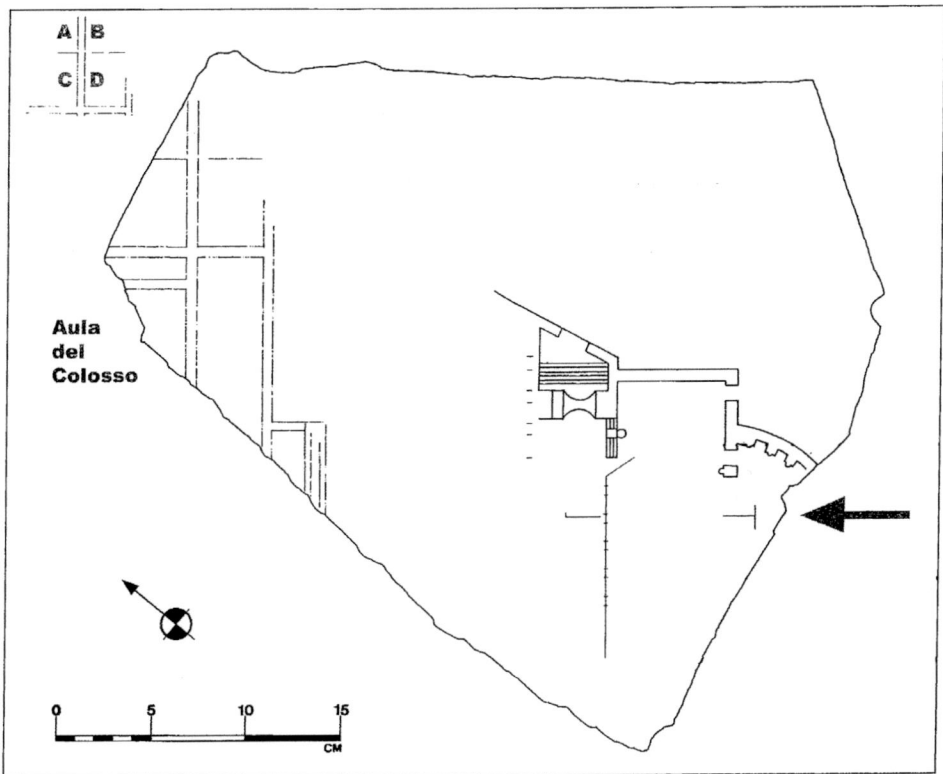

48.

1. Plan of the E section of the Forum of Augustus.
2. Walls pertinent to the NE part of the Forum of Augustus with the *aula* of the Colossus and the area *sub divo* between the N portico and the temple of Mars Ultor are represented. At the right, part of the S portico of the square, with the corresponding hemicycle and the arch of Germanicus are visible.
3. Found at Rome, in the SW area of the square of the *templum Pacis*, now in the Ufficio Fori Imperiali of the Soprintendenza BBCC of the Comune di Roma.
4. Severan age.
5. Slab of Luna marble.
6. Incision.
7. 41 x 35 cm.
8. Meneghini and Santangeli Valenzani (note 148) 29-30 and 157-195.

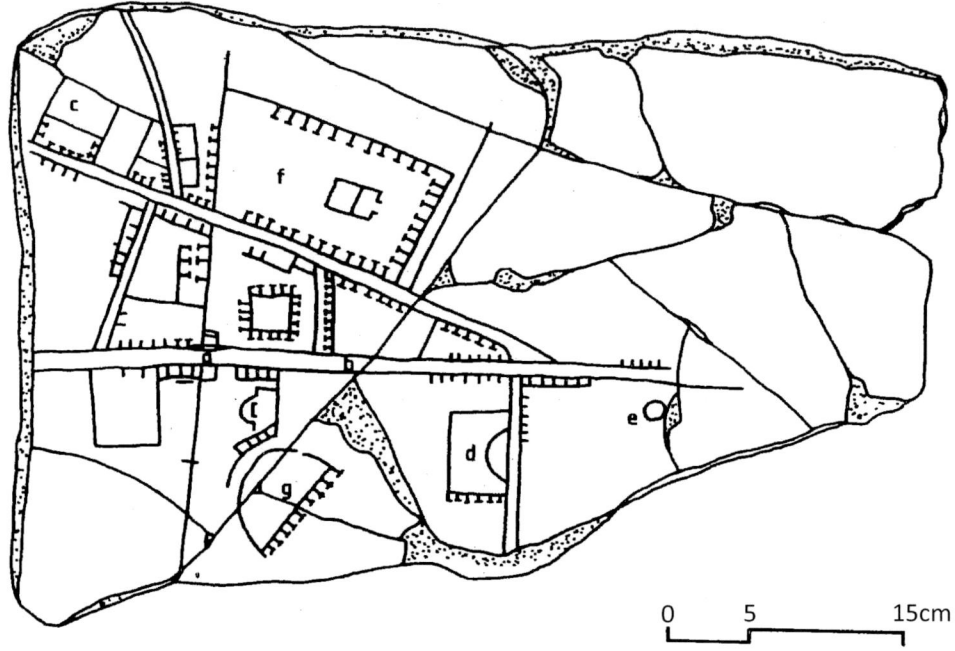

49.

1. Plan of the city of *Aguntum*.
2. In the context of the representation of the city of *Aguntum* the following elements of the city can be identified: the city walls (a), the decumanus (b), the baths (c), the curia (d), a round building – perhaps a *Nymphaeum* (e) -, the *Forum* with the temple (f) and the theatre (g).
3. Found in a post-ancient context of the ancient city of *Aguntum*. Now it is kept in the local Stadtmuseum.
4. Severan age.
5. Clay tile.
6. Incision.
7. 60 x 40 cm.
8. Heisel (note 109) 197.

9. CATALOGUE OF DRAWINGS OF ARCHITECTURES IN THE GREEK AND ROMAN WORLD

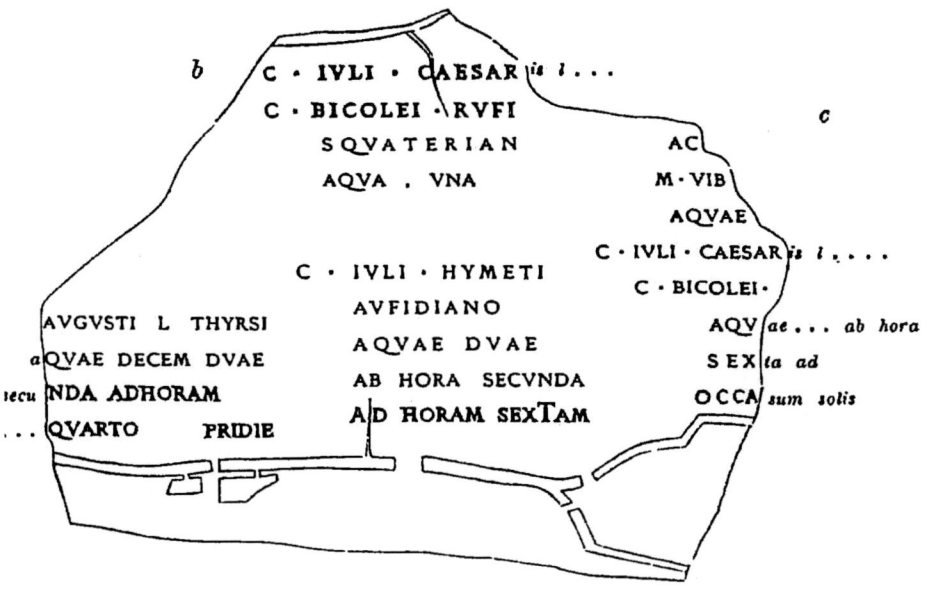

50.

1. Plan of aqueduct.
2. The route of an aqueduct is represented with indication of the sites and landowners in whose properties it was passing as well as of the times when it was possible to tap water.
3. *Quondam* at Rome, in the garden of the Church of St. Mary on the Aventinus hill.
4. Augustan or Julio-Claudian age.
5. Stone support.
6. Incision.
7. Dimensions not given.
8. Heisel (note 109) 185-186 and Haselberger, 'Architectural Likenesses' (note 110) 88.

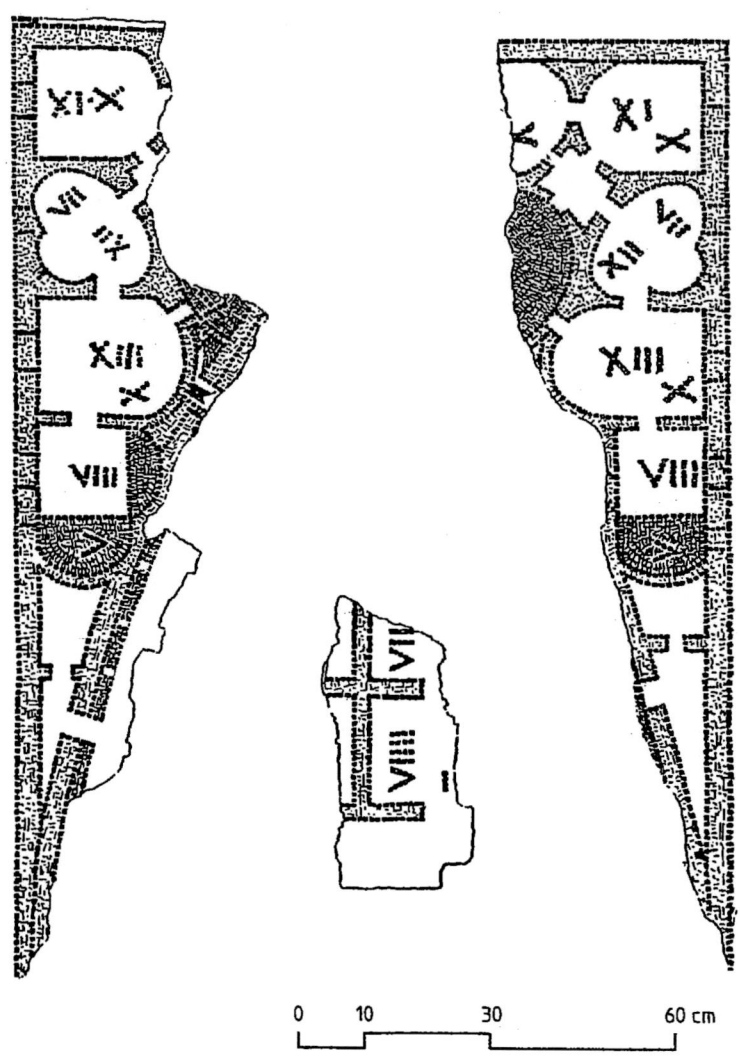

51.

1. Representation of baths.
2. The *balneum* where this mosaic stood is represented. In the preserved section there are traces of 19 rooms of the baths, with measures, given in feet, of lengths and widths.
3. Found at Rome, in Via Marsala, now in the Antiquarium of the Caelius hill.
4. Late Antonine Age.
5. Pavement.
6. Mosaic
7. 3, 40 x 5, 70 m.
8. Bouet and Meneghini and Santangeli Valenzani (note 152).

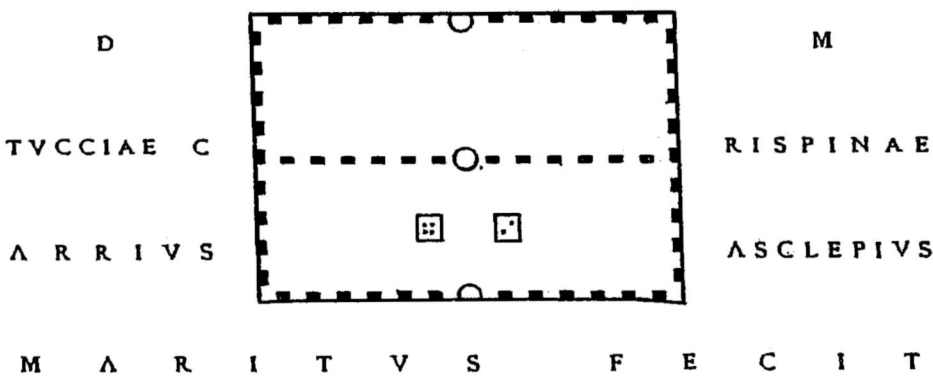

52.

1. Representation of sepulchral enclosure.
2. A rectangular sepulchral enclosure is represented, whose inner walls are endowed with rectangular elements which in maps of buildings of Roman age usually represent pillars. The two semicircles in the middle of the long sides of the rectangle perhaps represent the doorways. The line of smaller rectangles which divides the enclosure in two parts has been interpreted (Salza Prina Ricotti) as a line of trees, but usually trees in plans (see the example no. 41) are represented as round shaped dots. Thus it is much better to regard them small pillars which divided the courtyard above from the burial cell below. The small circle in the middle of the line of small rectangles may represent the doorway to the burial cell. In the latter there are two square bases above which there are, on the base at left, four steles, on the base at right, two steles. The inscription is the dedication of Arrius Asclepius to his wife Crispina.
3. Pavement mosaic of cubiculus adjacent to the sepulcher found at Ostia in a site named Monticelli, then in the Pacca collection. Three funerary steles were found in the sepulcher (*CIL* 14. 604-607).
4. Probably Severan age, because Crispina recorded in the inscription as wife of Arrius is probably Crispina wife of Arrius cited for the year 204 (*CIL* 6 add. 31707 and 32331). See P. Joers, 'Arrius 12-13', *RE* 2 (1896) 1255-1256 and G. Groeg, 'Crispinus 16', *ibidem* 4 (1901) 1271.
5. Pavement.
6. Mosaic.
7. 220 x 103 cm.
8. Heisel (note 153) and E. Salza Prina Ricotti, 'I giardini delle tombe', *Rendiconti Pontificia Accademia Archeologia* 76 (2003-2004) 231-261, particularly 233-234.

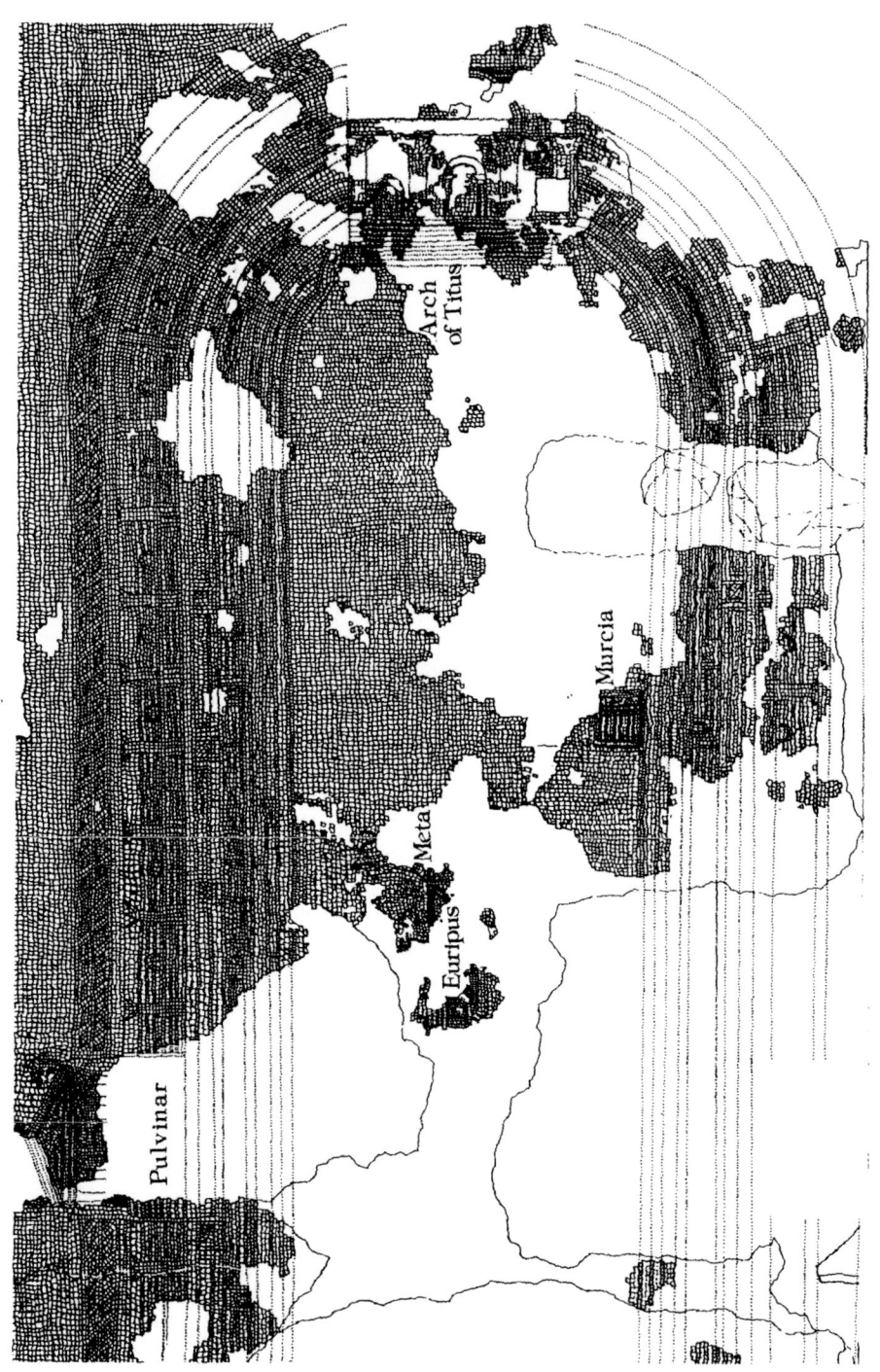

53.

53.

1. Drawing of a circus.
2. The plan of the hemicycle and of the near section of a circus is represented with indication of the steps, of the colonnade in *summa cavea*, of the *meta*, of the euripus, of the outer wall with the roof of the portico in *summa cavea*, of the arch with three fornixes in the middle of the hemicycle and of a small temple in the arena in the place corresponding to the small sanctuary of *Venus Murcia* in the *Circus Maximus*. This observation led to the identification of the architectural complex represented with the Circus Maximus.
3. Found at Luni, House of Mosaics.
4. Beginning of AD 5th century.
5. Pavement.
6. Mosaic.
7. 11, 2 x 3, 7 m.
8. Ciancio Rossetto (note 154) and moreover J. H. Humphrey, 'Two new Circus Mosaics', *AJA* 88 (1984) 392-397; Idem, *Roman Circuses*, London (1986) 243-244 and F. Marcattili, *Circo Massimo*, Rome (2009) 267, cat. no. 85.

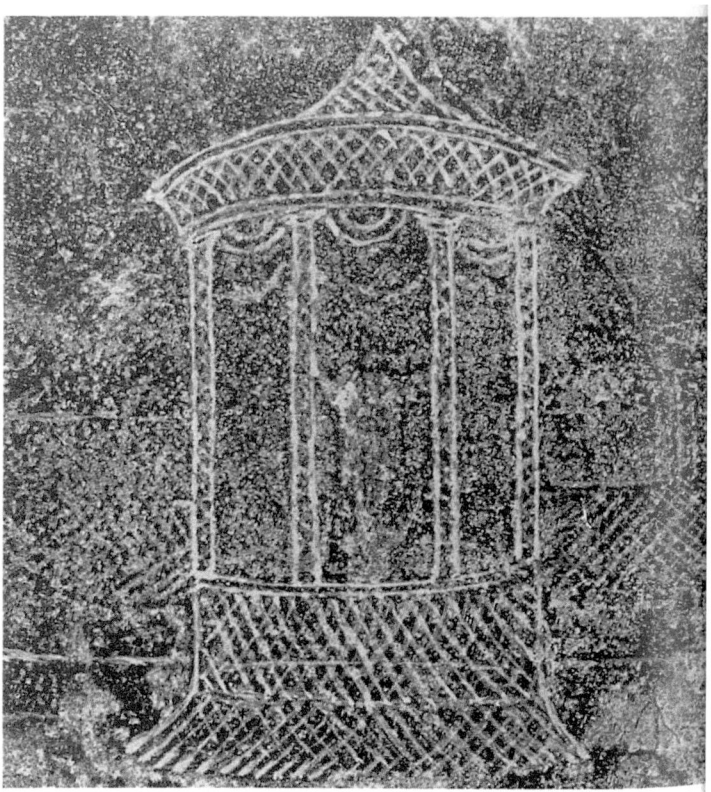

54.

1. Drawing of rotunda.
2. The rotunda is characterized from below by a podium having the shape of a truncated cone, by a cylindrical base and by a colonnade with very slender Doric columns, in whose intercolumns festoons are pending. The columns hold a flared ceiling on which a conic roof with concave surfaces stands. The image recalls the roof of a fountain at Baalbek (cat. no. 25) and may have represented a fountain or a pavilion or an aviary being similar to that described by Varro, *De re rustica* 3. 5. 8-17.
3. Pompeii, Casa del Citarista (= I 4, 5, 25), triclinium no. 19, S wall, E stretch, platform.
4. Julio-Claudian age.
5. Wall of triclinium.
6. Yellow colour on black ground.
7. Dimensions not given in the bibliography.
8. De Vos (note 155).

9. Catalogue of drawings of architectures in the Greek and Roman world

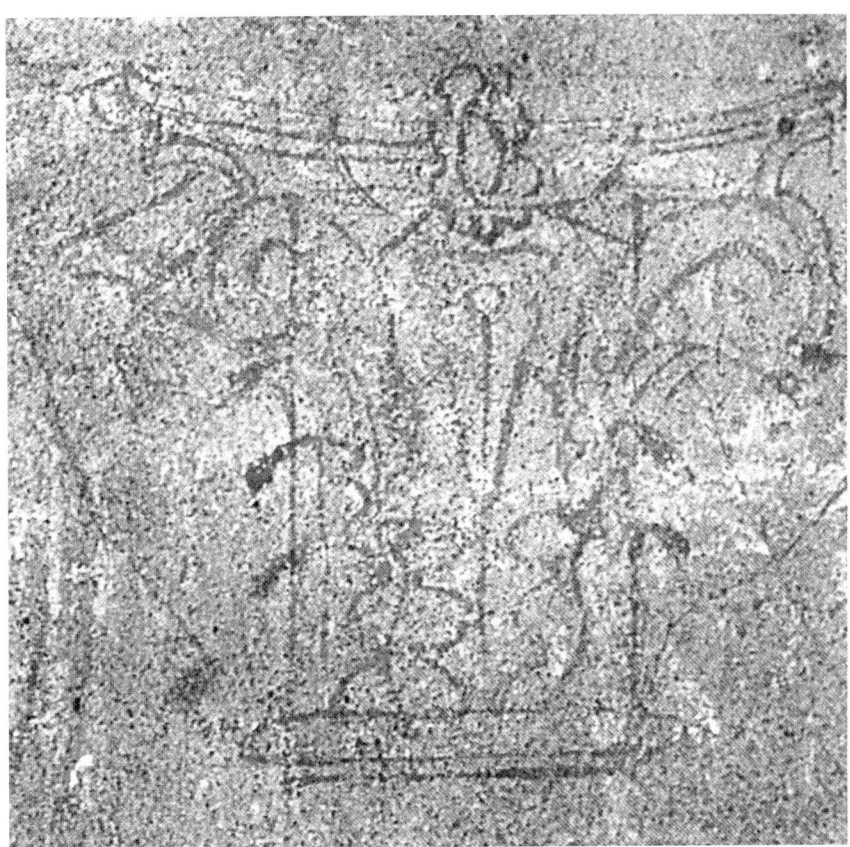

55.

1. Drawing of Corinthian capital.
2. A Corinthian capital is represented with indications of the upper collar of the upper shaft, of the shoots of acanthus, of the inner spirals, of the concave side of the abacus as well as of the flower in the middle of this side.
3. Pompei, Casa di Cerere, cubiculus k, S wall, central stretch.
4. Late 1st century BC.
5. Wall.
6. Red and yellow ochre on layer for the preparation of the plaster.
7. Dimensions not given.
8. De Vos (note 156).